VOICES of CAROLINA SLAVE CHILDREN

J. J. Smith Plantation, Beaufort County, S. C.
Courtesy, Library of Congress

VOICES OF CAROLINA SLAVE CHILDREN

compiled and edited by

NANCY RHYNE

SANDLAPPER PUBLISHING CO., INC.
Orangeburg, South Carolina

We are almost a nation of dancers, musicians and poets.

—Olaudah Equiano
From the Ibo tribe of Benin

Copyright © 1999 Nancy Rhyne

Front Cover Painting © Jonathan Green
　　　　Tales, 1988, Oil on Masonite, 24" x 36"
　　　　Jonathan Green — Naples, Florida

Published by Sandlapper Publishing Co., Inc.
　　　　Orangeburg, South Carolina

First Edition

Manufactured in the United States of America

Library of Congress Cataloging-in-Publication Data

Voices of Carolina slave children / [compiled by] Nancy Rhyne.
　　　p.　cm.
　　Includes bibliographical references.
　　ISBN 0-87844-150-6
　　1. Child slaves—South Carolina Biography.　2. Slaves—South
Carolina Interviews.　3. Afro-Americans—South Carolina Interviews.
4. Slavery—South Carolina—History—19th century.　5. Plantation
life—South Carolina—History—19th century.　6. South Carolina
Biography.　7. Oral history.　I. Rhyne, Nancy, 1926–
E445.S7V65　1999
975-7'00496073'00922—dc21
　　[B]　　　　　　　　　　　　　　　　99-28396
　　　　　　　　　　　　　　　　　　　CIP

PROLOGUE

Although it appears a blight on Carolina history, many would like to know more about the antebellum institution of slavery, which provided the means by which planters operated their huge tracts of land. Thousands of Africans, bought, sold, and maintained as property by their masters, managed to survive with the barest measure of autonomy. The narratives in this book give eyewitness accounts of some of those enslaved Africans who were children living in the Carolinas about the time of the Civil War.

Many of the Africans brought to North America landed at Charles Towne. Those placed on plantations in Carolina made up more than one-half of the colony's population. The planters and their families fled from the plantation "from frost to frost" in order to avoid the deadly malaria fever, a disease to which the Africans appeared immune. It may be said that the people who remained on the plantations year-round, producing the crops, were primarily responsible for the large fortunes made from indigo, sea island cotton, and rice.

Surely none of the Africans enjoyed enslavement and would rather have seen the Old South mansions laid in ruin and ash and had their freedom. But until emancipation came to them, they braced themselves and went about their work. They had greater knowledge than their masters of the daily tasks necessary to keep the plantation running, and certainly the planters realized that the people they kept in bondage were the most important element in the formula to success on their estates.

In 1935, in the midst of the Great Depression, Congress appropriated $4.8 million for the Works Projects Administration. This program, part of Roosevelt's New Deal, was designed to benefit the unemployed. WPA administrators generally assigned projects that utilized the skills of each individual hired. Laborers laid sewers; engineers designed and supervised the construction of bridges; office workers received assignments to white-collar projects; indigent actors arranged stages for plays; school teachers instructed thousands in shorthand, typing, English, and current events; artists painted portraits and landscapes; and writers recorded narratives of surviving enslaved Africans, people who worked in cotton mills, and thousands of others whose stories were deemed important enough to be kept in libraries for future reading, study, and reference. The Writers Project, as it is called today, is used extensively and praised by contemporary writers.

Agnes Tait became famous for her painting *Skating in Central Park*, which has been displayed at the National Museum of American Art in Washington, D.C. When contacted by WPA, Tait said, "I am working on a large decorative landscape of Central Park. My scene is that of a skating pond against the background of large buildings seen in the late afternoon light. Fortunately, the recent snows have afforded the effects I was seeking." Tait's painting captured the gaiety and commotion of the moment and even today evokes the feeling of a brisk, cold winter day. But for the WPA, the world might not have had that famous painting.

Hundreds of eyewitness accounts came from the work of the 2,250,000 people involved in the Works Projects Administration. For this book I consulted recorded WPA interviews with those individuals enslaved as children on North Carolina and South Carolina plantations. The stories give accurate accounts of their day-to-day activities. I have noted the name of the narrator and the plantation on which that person lived, when the information was available.

Stories of children in bondage are an essential part of the whole story of enslaved Africans in America. *Voices of Carolina Slave Children* seeks to present brief glimpses into the lives and customs of the children of that culture. Their descriptions of games, work, food, clothing, and thoughts about the Civil War, freedom, and 'mancipation parade across the pages in brilliant color.

Not all plantations were created equal, and some enslaved children had easier lives than others. It was my intention to select not only those stories of Africans who were happy but to include tales of those who did not find that period a paradise of kind masters, plentiful food, and carefree days. The WPA Writers Project accounts prove that, indeed, so many of the indentured people were unhappy they ran away. The suffering endured is clear in the pages that follow. The personalities and dispositions of the individuals interviewed vary greatly. While some enslaved men and women nearly buckled under hardships forced upon them, others offer a very different perspective on plantation life. I have tried to include interviews that cover the range of attitudes held by enslaved Africans.

As one reads the stories of emancipation, it is surprising to learn of the unexpected relief felt by some in bondage when told they could remain on the plantation. It must be taken into consideration that no preparation had been made for the Africans' freedom. Many of the newly freed had no place to go. They had no idea how or where they would obtain food. And they worried about who, if anyone, would take care of them when they were ill. As objectionable as enslavement was, many of the Africans chose to stay on with "Marse" and "Missus" rather than venture into the unknown.

Although these narratives have been edited for greater ease in reading, the voice remains true to the individual interviewed. I would like to make it unequivocally clear that the opinions and remembrances expressed in the narratives are those of individuals who endured enslavement, not those of historians.

I never knew an enslaved African, but I enjoyed a friendship with Sue Alston, a daughter of slaves, who lived and worked on Hampton Plantation, north of Charleston, until her death in 1985 at age 110. Sue told many stories of the Horrys, the Rutledges, and other masters and mistresses who lived in Hampton's fabled mansion, offering a remarkable view of the lifestyle of the Old South's millionaire planters. Sue's treasured words were published in 1997 in a book entitled *John Henry Rutledge: The Ghost of Hampton Plantation*.

For this book, I have gone to the people born in bondage, whose words have stripped away the glamour of life among the southern aristocrats and flung us straight to the hearts of the individuals who lived in "the quarters." Although they were adults at the time the narratives were recorded, these faithful souls revisited their childhoods in the telling of their stories. Some of the stories included here are the saddest I've ever heard; others are happy tales. But all draw the reader into the lives of those who lived outside the manor houses on Carolina plantations at the time of the Civil War.

It was my intention to include as many topics as possible regarding the lives of children on Carolina plantations before, during, and after the Civil War. Most of the stories were told in dialect, and for that reason I have edited them in order to make them more accessible to the general reader. A glossary is provided as an aid in understanding the speech.

The narratives that follow offer a perspective of the institution of slavery, the Civil War, and the Carolinas that has appeared in few history books.

As with many of my other books, research material for *Voices of Carolina Slave Children* came from the Library of Congress in Washington, D.C., and the South Caroliniana Library on the University of South Carolina campus in Columbia, S.C.

Nancy Rhyne
Myrtle Beach, S.C.

For

Dr. Willie L. Harriford ∾ *South Carolina Board of Education (Ret.)*
who warned me, "Some will feel that any discussion of slavery should be omitted because it was a painful period of time, but this lack of discussion leaves everyone misinformed."

and for

Maya Angelou ∾ *poet, playwright, professor, author, actress, and director*
who said of slavery, "I'm saddened when I hear people, even the black community, say: 'Let's forget that stuff, let's move ahead.' We can only know where we're going if we know where we've been." Dr. Angelou holds up as her thesis: "You may encounter many defeats, but you must not be defeated."

Acknowledgements ────────────────────────────────

I am grateful to **Thomas Elmore**, retired teacher, Myers Park High School, Charlotte, North Carolina, and **Teresa Burns**, teacher, Aynor Elementary School, Aynor, South Carolina, who gave me invaluable advice on how the stories in this book can be especially effective when used in the classroom.

My heartfelt thanks to **Chris Stanley** of Bay Street Trading Company, Beaufort, South Carolina, for introducing me to Jonathan Green's beautiful artwork and placing in my hands a copy of *Tales*, which she proclaimed the perfect image for the cover of the book.

I'd like to thank **Jonathan Green Studios** for allowing us to use *Tales*, to give *Voices of Carolina Slave Children* the perfect face.

My gratitude to **Amanda Gallman** and **Barbara Stone** of Sandlapper Publishing who worked with me to bring this special book to life.

And, finally, to my husband Sid, my love and appreciation for your continued support of my work.

VOICES OF CAROLINA SLAVE CHILDREN

They Say I Was Found In A Basket

Where was I born? Well, that'll take some hearsay. I never knew my mammy. They say I was found in a basket, dressed in nice baby clothes, on the railroad track. The engineer stopped the train, got out, and found me something like the princess found Moses, but not in the bulrushes. The conductor took care of me until the train reached Dawkins Station, where Marse Tom Dawkins came to meet the train that morning. When he first laid eyes on me, he claimed I belonged to him. He said he had the right to me, and the conductor didn't object to that 'cause little African boys were owned in that day and time. Not free 'til 'mancipation. Marse Tom carried me home and gave me to his wife, Missus Betsy. She named me John and became my mistress. People would look at me and say, "Who's that?" "Oh, that's John." "John who?" "Just John."

Marse Tom Dawkins had a fine mansion. He owned all the land around Dawkins Station. When I became a boy, Missus Betsy told me she believed that Sheton Brown was my pappy. On that day I took the name of Brown and became John Brown.

When the war came on, Marse Richard, the overseer, shouldered his gun and as he was educated more than most of the white folks, he rose to be captain in the Confederate Army. It's a pity he got killed in that war.

The Yankees came and burned Marse Tom's mansion, the gin house, and the mill. They took all the sheep, mules, cows, hogs, and even the chickens. They set we Africans free. We were *free*.

JOHN BROWN
DAWKINS STATION, S. C.

Big Ole Long Frock

Girls in the big house wear long ole frock in that time. They used to wear them big ole hoop skirt that sit out broad-like from the ankle and then they wear little panty that show 'tween their skirt and their ankle. Just tie panty 'round their knees with some sorta string and let them show that way 'bout their ankles. I 'member we black chillun go into the woods and get wild grape vine and stand it out like big hoop. Have a smaller hoop closer to the waist. Never have hoop in the waist 'cause that was s'posed to be little bitty thing. Frocks on the plantation were made of pretty cloth.

They weave cloth right there on the plantation. Wear cotton and woolens in that time. 'Course the Missus could go and get the finest kind of silk cause most of her thing come from abroad. My ole mammy worked that spinning wheel. She sat there at the old spinning wheel and took one shuttle and threw it one way and then another the other way and pull that string and make it tighter and tighter. She had to work her feet too. That was the way they made cloth in that day and time.

MAGGIE BLACK
MARION, S. C.

I Was The Houseboy

My master was Marse Jim Stewart and my Missus was his wife, Missus Clara. They lived in a fine house 'bout two miles southwest of Winnsboro. My mother was the cook and I was the houseboy.

On that plantation were many two-room houses, brick chimneys in the middle, for the plantation Africans. In the growin' season I go with Marse every day, not to drive, too small for that, just to hold the horse when he got out, and then I ran errands for him, 'round the house and in the fields.

Marse liked hound dogs and I liked a hound dog. That kind of breed had a good nose and made a good 'possum dog. Marse told me one time that the first dog sprung from a wolf, and that first dog was a hound dog. I followed his talk with belief 'bout the setters, pointers, and bloodhounds, but that belief was strained when it came down to the little useless pups the ladies lead 'round with a silver collar and shiny chain.

ALEXANDER ROBERTSON
WINNSBORO, S. C.

It Makes Me Tremble To Talk About That

Pappy and Mammy belonged to Marse Sam Louie who had a big plantation in Calhoun County. He had 'bout fifty or more grown Africans besides many African chillun. Old Marse raised big crops and saved what he made. He sure was a fine business man but he was mighty hard on everybody. He told his Africans to work hard and make him a heap of money and he would keep it in case of hard times.

When news spread that the Yankees were coming to free the Africans, he called all us up in the yard and showed us a big sack of money. He said he was going to kill all the Africans before the Yankees set us free and that we wouldn't need any money after we were dead. All us Africans were sad and troubled. It makes me tremble to talk about that, but Providence was walking 'round the plantation that day and night. It was whispered 'round that old Marse had come down with smallpox. They buried him two days after that.

After old Marse flew away, everything was different on the plantation. Missus Nancy, old Marse's wife, told us Africans that when the Yankees freed us, we could stay right there and work on shares or by the day, whichever we wanted. Me and my folks stayed on with Missus Nancy, but we were free.

ISOM ROBERTS
CALHOUN COUNTY, S. C.

Little As I Was, I Had A Notion

My mammy and pappy lived on Marse Frank Jeffries' place. Pappy was the stableman and a good horseman. Mammy worked at the big house, working the weaving machine. It went plop, plop as she treaded it with her feet. I picked up twigs, swept the yard, and such as that. Marse Frank didn't go to the war 'cause he was too old.

One day the Yankees came. They were thick as hornets, coming down the road in a cloud of dust. They tied their horses and tied Marse Frank to the porch railings. I got a butcher knife so I could free Marse Frank, but a Yankee snatched the knife and told me to stick out my tongue, he was going to cut it off. I let out a yell and ran out of the house.

Just then I saw the bee gums in the side yard. Little as I was, I had a notion. I got me a long stick and turned over every bee gum, and that stirred up the bees. You never saw the like of bees. They swarmed all over the place. As the Yankees came out of the house, carrying Missus Mary Jane's fine furniture, mirrors, and glassware, them bees sailed into them Yankees like bullets. The Yankees put down the treasure, ran to their horses and lit out. Missus Mary Jane and Marse Frank said, "Ida Lee, if you hadn't turned over the bee gums, the Yankees would've toted off everything we own."

IDA LEE ADKINS
UNION COUNTY, S. C.

My First 'Membrance Is A Dream

I was born ten years before freedom on Christmas Day. My first 'membrance is a dream. I thought I saw my little sister, Sara, lying on a cooling board. I was five years old at that time. I woke my mother up and told her 'bout it, but it was just a dream and wasn't nothing to it.

My grandfather had a prayer meeting house. All the African folks on the plantation went to it every Saturday night. They sat on benches, and then they would get down on their knees and pray. I was a little gal, and me and the other gals would fetch water for them to drink. We toted pine wood for the stove, and we'd take coals 'round for the old folks to light their pipes with. After a while they got to singing and shouting. Then the Spirit come down and took hold of them. That would be when everybody would get happy. The old rafters creaked and shook as the Spirit of the Lord sank deeper and deeper in the hearts of the praying folks.

I nursed when I was a little gal. Mammy made me make teas to cure folks' colds and ailments. She made me fetch her water and towels and other things while she waited on the sick folks. That's the way I broke into nursing at Monarch Plantation. When the flu passed on and the folks got well, they paid me for my services.

LINA ANNE PENDERGRASS
MONARCH PLANTATION
CHESTER COUNTY, S. C.

Corn Bread Was As Sweet
As Pound Cake Ever Been

Marse gave every African family a peck of meal and a quart of syrup and so much meat every week and allowed them all to have a garden. Mammy and Pappy worked the garden by moonshine, 'cause in the morning they had to do Marse's work.

I tell you corn bread was as sweet to me in that day and time as pound cake ever been. Wasn't any picking and choosing about nothing. We ate right smart 'possums and rabbits. I caught them when the water swelled and the animals came out of the woods to hunt dry land. They couldn't conceal themselves in the open fields, and that is how come I catched them so easy.

People came to big dinners and to dance in the big house. I toted water from the kitchen to the dining room, and I fixed up that room with trimmings. Got pine and cedar limbs and put over the pictures and around the mantle boards. Marse and Missus served their friends eggnog in the winter and mint juleps in the summer. Sometimes there was syllabub. This is how the mens picked out the pretty gals for to dance with: They wrote down their name and handed it to me. I went to the gal and dropped a curtsy and handed her the name. If she wanted to dance with him, she looked at him and flicked her fan, and if she didn't want to dance she never gave him no mind.

ROB PERRY
JIM PERRY PLANTATION
EDGEFIELD COUNTY, S. C.

We Were All Together After Freedom

Marse Gene and Missus Gracie had two chillun: we called them Marse Willis and Missus Rhoda. I started working in the field. It sure made me hungry. I remember how I'd get a tin cupful of pot liquor from the greens, crumble cornbread in it and enjoy it as the bestest part of the dinner. We never suffered for something to eat, but not have the best of clothes. I go all summer in my shirttail and in the winter I had to do the best I could, without any shoes. But I liked to go barefooted.

My pappy got a pass and came to see my mammy and me every Saturday night. Marse Willis' Africans were about eight women, and their husbands came from other plantations to marry them and have chillun. I don't remember nary one of the women having a husband living with her every night. Houses were made of logs, cup and saddled at both ends, and covered with white oak board shingles. Had stick and mud chimneys.

When the Yankees came, they got so mad when they couldn't find any salt they burned up everything, just made a clean sweep. Then Freedom came, and Marse leave. Sold out. We went to Walhalla and moved in with Pappy. We were all together after freedom.

CHARLIE ROBINSON
JOE BEARD PLANTATION
FAIRFIELD COUNTY, S. C.

I Knew 'Bout The Civil War

I knew 'bout the Civil War. I was young lad when the big gun shoot and the Yankees pile down from the North. Talk 'bout being brave. The bravest thing I ever saw was one at Ashepoo Junction. Grant was standing up before Richmond; Sherman was marching tump-tump-tump through Georgia. I got to see and hear everything. One day the overseer sent Pappy to Ashepoo Junction to get the mail. I went with him. The train start to come in. What a lot of train! The air was smoked up with all them soldiers, going off to war. They came shouting in from Charleston, bound for the Up Country.

I stood with Pappy near the long trestle, and saw the train rock by. One engine in front pulled, and one in the back pushed, pushed, pushed. The train was loaded down with soldiers. They were as thick as peas, riding on the roof, shouting and hollering. I make big amaze to see such a lot of soldiers—all going down to die. And they started to sing as they crossed the trestle. One picked a banjo; one played the fiddle. They sang and whooped, they laughed; they hollered to the people on the ground and sang out, "Good-bye." All going down to die.

WILLIAM ROSE
PETER'S POINT PLANTATION
EDISTO ISLAND, S. C.

I Was Sold So Much

I really don't know who my first Marse was, 'cause I was sold so much. I reckon I was born in Beaufort County, and the first time I was sold I was in my Mammy's arms. We were sold to a man in Charleston and then I was sold to Marse McKee, and that's the first thing I remember.

Marse McKee was mean to us, and we never had anything for ourselves. He owned three hundred Africans and he had four overseers. I worked in the big house, 'round the table. When word came that I was to be sold again I was glad as I could be. Then they told me that Marse McKee had gambled and had lost me to a Marse Hartman. Marse Hartman was good as he could be. When his overseers were cruel, he let them go.

Marse and Missus Mary left to go to the mountains, and soon after that the war broke out. We stayed on the plantation during the war, and when the war was about over, Marse Hartman and Missus Mary came home. The Africans still loved them and we all went over and cleaned the house and fixed it up.

CHANEY SPELL
BEAUFORT COUNTY, S. C.

"Hoppin' John and Limpin' Lizzie"

My name is Welcom Beese, and I lived at Oatland Plantation. I can't tell you the day I was born, but Marse took it down. Mammy had twelve head of chillun born at Oatland Plantation. Marse bought my mammy in Virginia. Her name was Dolly. Sam was her husband's name. When Mammy was bought, she was a young woman. She worked in rice. She always said, "I work in rice at Oatland." She did that all right. She plowed the rice in April. At the harvest in late summer, Mammy cut the rice with a scythe and allowed it to dry on the stubble for three days. Then she tied it in sheaves and it was taken to the stableyard. A lot of money was made on rice. I minded the horses. Marse had plenty of horses. We ate a lot of "Hoppin' John" and "Limpin' Lizzie." "Hoppin' John" is peas and rice cooked together, and "Limpin' Lizzie" is peas and hominy cooked together.

WELCOM BEESE
OATLAND PLANTATION
GEORGETOWN COUNTY, S. C.

All Disease Started
When Female Ate The Apple In Eden

Marse was a kind and tender man to his Africans. You see, he was a man who loved horses and animals. Well, that's the way he loved us, though maybe in a bigger portion. Marse John never married. He was good enough to buy my old grandmammy Mary, though she never could do much work. I guess Marse John had forty Africans. We lived in two-story log houses with plank floors.

I remember about the war for freedom. Some of the Africans were sent to the front to use pick and shovel to throw up breastworks. Marse went to war and Pappy carried on at home. He was the foreman. Dr. Scott was our doctor. There were rattlesnake bites and people had lots of chills and fever. They were way off about what made chills and fever come on you. Some allowed it was a miasma that the devil brought around you from the swamp and settled around your face while you slept. Marse found out that the mosquito brought the fever and chills, and he allowed it was the female mosquito bite that did the business. I didn't believe that at first, 'til the doctor told me that it was no harder to believe than to believe that all disease came into the world when a female took a bite of the apple in the garden of Eden.

REUBEN ROSBORO
FAIRFIELD PLANTATION
RIDGEWAY, S. C.

Margaret One

Pappy, Michael One, was the principal plantation carpenter and they gave him the name of One because of that. We lived on Wachesaw Plantation, on the Waccamaw River. Mammy, Mary One, dyed cloth with indigo and black walnut bark. She had to weave day and night to make up that cloth. I, Margaret One, say, "Where Mammy?" They say, "Mammy to the weaving house." She sailed along with that shuttle. Michael One, my twin brother, got his name from Pappy. Auntie Ritta One, Pappy's sister, nurse all the chillun while their mammies and pappies in the rice field. All size chillun. Auntie give them the gypsy [gypsum] weed when they infected with worm. She give them the gypsy weed when the moon change. When the moon changed, she did that.

I was born with a caul over my face. That means I can see the spirit [ghosts]. And I saw the Yankee.

When a whole gang of Yankee came they caught a fowl and tell me, "Little gal, go in the house!" I went home and didn't come out that day. The moon shine like day that night. Yankee spent the night in the Doctor House, where the sick folks were. The next day the Yankee left the plantation.

Margaret One
Wachesaw Plantation

We Plant By the Signs

When I was little bitty gal we plant by the signs. Plant peas, peanuts, bunch snap beans, bunch sieve beans, cucumber, and turnips on full of the moon. Plant running sieve beans in March. If tall okra was wanted, a child planted that. It grew fast like the child what planted it. If dwarf okra was wanted, a grown person planted that and it grew slow. If very hot pepper was wanted, a person with much temper planted that and the pepper was red hot. We plant no vegetables when the wind was a-comin' from the east. If you did that, bugs and worms destroyed them. Plant them on dark nights.

ELIZABETH MIDDLETON
CHARLESTON COUNTY, SOUTH CAROLINA

The Tar Baby Story

All the chillun on the plantation on the Pee Dee River liked the tar baby story. It didn't come out the same way every time, but this is how it went when Mammy set me down and told it to me:

Buh Wolf say, "Who muddy my water?" Buh Wolf ask Buh Rabbit and Buh 'Gator and Buh Fox.

Now you see Buh Rabbit done slip down there and muddy the spring water, but Buh Rabbit say he don't know who did it.

So Buh Wolf make him a tar baby and stand him up down there by the spring. And the next morning early Buh Rabbit went hopping down to the spring. Bright and early. He saw this little gal standing there. Say, "Good morning, little gal." Little gal wouldn't crack. Wouldn't crack her mouth. He say, "Good morning," three times. Little gal wouldn't tell a thing. So he hauled off and slapped her.

Buh Rabbit's hand stuck to the gal. "Turn me loose, little gal! I slap you again." So he hauled off and slapped her with the other hand. "Turn me loose, little gal! Turn me loose!" With both hands stuck, Buh Rabbit kick with one foot. That foot stuck. "Turn me loose!" He kick with other foot, and it stuck too. Little gal wouldn't turn him loose. He say he'll take the head and butt her. He butt and the head stuck tight. He begged and begged, but the little gal wouldn't turn him loose.

Buh Wolf come. Buh Rabbit all huddled up, all doubled over, buckled over. All his hands fastened and his head fastened and his feet fastened. He was huddled over the tar baby. Buh Wolf say, "Ah, ha. I found out who was muddying my spring. Buh Rabbit, what must I do with you? I don't know whether to throw you in the fire and burn you up or throw you in the briar patch."

Buh Rabbit make out like he was not particular about the fire, but he begged like he thought the briar patch was terrible. Buh Wolf say, "I'll throw you in the briar patch." "Please don't!"

So Buh Wolf take Buh Rabbit and jerk him loose from the tar baby and pitch him over in the briar patch just like he was going to stave him against the thorns of the briar and punish him. And Buh Rabbit holler out, "Thank God! I right where I born and raised at! I raised in the briar patch."

PHILLIPA KNOX
GEORGETOWN COUNTY, S. C.

The Most I Had To Do
Was Keep The House Clean

I was born right down at Cedar Creek, in Fairfield County. Marse was Samuel Black and Missus was Martha. They had five chillun, and they lived in a great big house up on a hill. It was right pretty. There were forty of us Africans in all and it took all of us to keep the plantation going. Most Africans worked in the fields. They went to work as soon as it got light enough to see how to get around; when twelve o'clock came, they all stopped for dinner and didn't go back to work 'til two. They worked on 'til it got almost dark.

After the crops were all gathered, there was still plenty of work to do. I stayed in the house with the white folks. The most I had to do was to keep the house cleaned up and nurse the chillun. I had a heap of pretty clothes to wear, 'cause Missus gave me her old clothes. Sometimes I was bad. One time Missus went off on a visit and left me at home. When she came back, Sally told her that I had put on a pair of Marse's pants and scrubbed the floor with them on. Missus told me it was a sin for me to put on a man's pants, and she whipped me pretty bad. She said it's in the Bible that a man shall not put on a woman's clothes, or a woman put on man's clothes. I never put on pants after that.

Marse and Missus never taught us to read nor write. They taught us our ABCs, and to read some in the testament, but one African learned enough to write his pass and ran away and went up North.

VICTORIA ADAMS
COLUMBIA, S. C.

They Were Too Highfalutin' In Their Ways

My color wasn't allowed to go to the white folks' church. No African was welcome there. Thinking as how I was bright enough to get in, I up and went there one Sunday. How they did bow and scrape and ape the white folks. I saw some pretty feathers, fans, and women there, but I was uncomfortable all the time 'cause they were too highfalutin in their ways, in their singing, and all sorts of carrying on.

Marse was James Barber. He went to the war for 'mancipation and then he came home. I learned all I could about that war. I thought Abe Lincoln was a poor buckra. Although Marse Lincoln meant well, I can't help but wish he had continued splittin' them fence rails, which they say he knew all about, and never took a hand in running the government of which he knew nothing about. Marse Jeff Davis was all right, but he shoulda gone to the war and fought like General Lee and General Jackson.

ED BARBER
WINNSBORO, S. C.

Marse Had A System Of Bells

"The Old Squire," as Marse Matthew Peterson Hayes was called, was an outstanding man, and in the dress of that antebellum period, wearing his silk beaver, he was well-known as a leader. His system of bells was very unusual. He had small bells of different tones for various servants, all kept in a row on his desk. John, the driver, knew his bell, and so did Anthony, and the gardener and the yard man. Marse had whistles for the chickens, geese, ducks, turkeys, guineas, and pigeons. At feeding time he went to each coop and blew the whistle, and the fowl came to his call. Some of the pigeons were not afraid to light on his shoulder.

A large house in the yard was used as a hospital for sick Africans. Marse and his own family cared for them. I remember Marse looking at his watch and giving the medicine. Babies were kept in the place called the hospital, a big white house near the quarters.

Marse took some of his favorite Africans to his church where a special service was held under a large arbor in summer. We sat in the gallery. Daddy Marcus was the sexton of that church, and Case helped out.

Marse's carriage just light up my eyes, with the coachman in front, separated from the family by glass, and the brass carpeted steps which let down from the side doors.

PHOEBE
HAYESVILLE, S. C.

The Milliner Was A Yankee

I cleaned up the big house for Marse Dr. Thomas Leslie Burgess and my Missus. Sometimes I cooked for them. I remember when a milliner for the best store in Maryland came to stay in the big house. One Sunday morning, before they all left for church, Missus said not to go into the milliner's room until she came out and then go in and clean it up. But I went in before the milliner came out, and she said her people from the North were going to come South and free my people. She carried on so. I didn't know she was a Yankee until then! I carried what she said in my breast 'til church was over and Marse and Missus and the milliner came home.

I met them in the yard and asked Missus, "Did you know she is a Yankee?" "Yes," said Missus, "she is a mighty nice Yankee and we all love her." "Ain't you 'fraid she will burn the house down?" I question. "Oh, no. She is our friend, and we love her. She is a good Yankee." I said, "I dunno. I go in the room to clean up and she tell me her people free me and ain't I glad. And I said no, I wish her people would let me alone." And the milliner said to me, "You are free now. You don't have such hard work." And then she said to Missus, "I am amazed to find the love she has in her heart for you. I believe your Africans are happier now than they will be after we set them free." We were happy, and we took the name Burgess after we were set free.

PHYLLIS BURGESS
CLARENDON COUNTY, S. C.

At Night I Carded And Spinned On Missus's Wheels

We had plenty good house to live in and some fair things to eat like squirrels, rabbits, 'possums, birds, fatback, turnips, cabbages, cornbread, milk, and pot liquor. Marse sent his corn, apples, and peaches to old man Scruggs at Helena, near Newberry, to have him make whiskey, brandy, and wine. Old man Scruggs was good at that business.

In the winter I didn't have much clothes, and no shoes. At night I carded and spinned on Missus's wheels, helping Mammy. Then an old woman weaved the cloth. I worked in the big house, washed, ironed, cleaned up and was nurse when the war was going on. When I was sick, Dr. Ruff attended to me. I remember he traveled on a horse, with saddle bags behind him. He made his own medicines.

We didn't have a chance to learn to read and write. I saw Africans sold on the block; saw a mammy and her little infant was taken away from her and sent away. Families were separated from each other, some going to one white missus and some to another.

Marse was most always mean to us. He got mad spells and whipped like the mischief.

G. BLUFORD
NEWBERRY, S. C.

21

All Us Chillun Ate With Mussell Shells

I, Mary, was born on a plantation near Franklinton, Wake County, North Carolina, on May 10, 1851. I belonged to Sam Brodie, who owned the plantation; Missus's name was Evaline. My pappy was Alfred and Mammy was Bertha. We had good food, plenty of home-made clothes and the African houses were in a section called the quarters. African houses had two rooms. Marse and Missus lived in what was called the Great House, located in a large grove one mile square covered with oak and hickory trees. It had twelve rooms.

In winter, ice was gathered and kept in a deep hole in the ground and covered. A large frame building was built over it. There was a door and steps leading down to the bottom of the hole. Certain foods were kept down there. Everything we used was made on the plantation. There was a grist mill, tannery, shoe shop, blacksmith shop, and looms for weaving cloth.

There were about sixty-two Africans on the plantation, and every Sunday morning all us chillun had to be bathed, dressed, and our hair combed and carried down to the Great House for breakfast in order that Marse and Missus could watch us and pick out the sickly ones. All of us chillun carried a mussel shell to eat with. The food was on large trays, and we all gathered around and ate, dipping up our food with the mussel shells, which we used for spoons. Those who refused to eat had to come back to the Great House for their meals and medicine until they were well.

Marse taught us chillun to be obedient in a nice quiet way. We were taught to take our hats and bonnets off before going into the Great House, and to bow and say, "Good morning Marse and Missus Evaline." Patrollers were not allowed on the place unless they came peacefully, and I never knew of them whipping any Africans on Marse's place. Everybody got biscuits on Sundays. African women went to Marse for their Sunday allowance of flour. All the chillun would be in the Great House, eating breakfast. We were allowed to have prayer meeting in our homes in the quarters, and sometimes we went to the white folks' church. Marse and Missus would not teach any of us to read and write. Books and papers were forbidden. Marse's chillun and the African chillun played together.

During the war for 'mancipation, news went from plantation to plantation, and while the Africans acted natural, some even more polite than usual, they prayed for freedom. Then one day I heard something that sounded like thunder and Missus and Marse began to walk around and act funny. Grown Africans whispered to each other. The next day I heard it again, boom, boom, boom. I asked Missus if it was going to rain, and she said, "Mary, go to the icehouse and bring me some pickles and preserves." I went and got them. She ate a little and gave me some. Then she said, "You run along and play."

In a day or two everybody on the plantation seemed to be disturbed and Marse and Missus were crying. Marse ordered all the Africans to come to the Great House at nine o'clock. They walked toward the Big House from every direction. You could have heard the breast feather of a chicken fall, it was so quiet. Marse said, "Good morning," and Missus said, "Good morning." Then Marse said, "Men, women and chillun, you are free. You are no longer my Africans. The Yankees will soon be here." Marse and Missus went into the house and got two large chairs and put them on the porch facing the avenue of oak trees and sat down side-by-side and watched.

In about an hour there was one of the blackest clouds coming up the avenue from the main road. It was the Yankee soldiers, and they filled the long avenue that reached to the Great House. The Yankees dismounted. They called to us Africans and said, "You are free." We all started whooping and laughing and acting like we were crazy. Yankee soldiers shook hands with us. Then they began to take what they wanted. They busted the door to the smoke house and got all the hams and then went to the icehouse. They found several barrels of brandy. Finally, they made fires and cooked.

Marse and Missus were still sitting on the porch. They were so humble that no Yankee did anything to the Big House. When the Yankees left, a lot of the Africans went with them, and soon there were none of Marse's people left.

MARY ANDERSON
WAKE COUNTY, N. C.

I Attended My Own Funeral

Missus took me as a little pet. My name was Rose, and she called me her "Rose of Sharon," a plant what's mentioned in the Bible. Talk about the Bible, I always liked to hold the Bible when I was a little bitty praying girl. I spent some time thinking about my funeral, and I wanted to attend it to see who my friends were. Missus told me not to think about that so much.

Marse planted cotton, corn, peas, and potatoes and we had plenty to eat. I hardly ever feel sad, but I felt sad during the war and I thought about my funeral. Just before the Yankees came, Marse and Missus left the plantation. When the Yankees came, I saw them galloping to the house, canteen boxes on their hips and bayonets rattling by their sides. They searched the house, and then they got all us Africans together and made us sing "Gimme That Old-Time Religion." They sent us for chickens, which we killed and fried. Then they burned the smokehouse but didn't burn the big house.

ROSE
UNION, S. C.

NOTE: Many years after freedom, Rose wished her funeral preached before her death to ascertain the esteem of her friends. Her old marse granted her wish, and she attended her own funeral, held in front of her cabin in the quarters, which was just as she had left it after freedom came.

Confederate Soldiers Near End Of Civil War

I was a little shirttail boy when the Confederate soldiers were going from house to house with packs on their backs. They needed everything—socks, gloves, food—but they were the awfullest looking white folks us African chillun had ever seen. They set up camp at Marse Bill Oxner's place in Goshen Hill and they never had anything in their packs but a few old rags and little keepsakes from the women folks who loved them back home. Their hair was long and stringy and all matted around the face and neck. 'Cause in them days, all the fine white men wore beards, 'cause that was the fashion. But them soldiers' beards looked worse than their hair. Their faces carried the awfullest look what you have ever seen on any man's face. Their clothes looked worse that any clothes had ever looked before the war. None of them had garments that fit them. Us African chillun looked out and said, "Yonder comes some more of them old lousy soldiers."

BELLAM LYLES
UNION, S. C.

"The Prince Of Wales Gave Me This Box."

My Missus was a daughter of Anne Jane Neil, who lived to be a hundred and five years old, and it is written on her tombstone in the cemetery. Old Missus Anne Jane Neil was born in Ireland, across the ocean. She had a silver snuff box. She'd take snuff out of that box, rub it up her nose and say, "The Prince of Wales gave me this box before I came to this country, and I was presented to Queen Victoria by the Duke of Wellington on my sixteenth birthday." She claimed she was born over there the very night of the battle of Waterloo. And she would go on and allow that when the duke took her by the hand and led her up to the queen, he said, "Your majesty, this young lady was born on the night of our great victory at Waterloo."

My Missus was Missus Margaret. I was given to her when she was married to Marse Wade Brice. I was five years old and went along with them to Woodward, South Carolina. Mammy gave me to them at that time. We lived in Marse Wade's quarters. There was a row of log houses, with chimneys made of sticks and mud, but the floor was a good plank floor. The bed was a wood bedstead with a wheat straw mattress of good ticking. There were no windows to the house, so it was warm in the winter and blue blazing hot in summer. Our clothes consisted of woolens in the winter and a one-piece slip-on in the summer. All us Africans went to church at Concord twice every month and learned the shorter catechism.

After Missus died, Marse marry Missus Tilda Watson, a perfect angel, if there ever was one on this red earth. She took a liking to me right at the jump, on first sight. I nursed all her chillun and shooed the flies off the table with a fan made out of peacock feathers. Marse went off to the war and got shot in the hip, but he joined the Calvary soon after and was away when the Yankees came through. The Yankees burned and stole everything on the place. They took off all the sheep, mules, and cows; killed all the hogs; caught all the chickens, ducks, and geese; and shot the turkeys and tied them to their saddles as they left.

PHINIE STEWART
BLACKSTOCK, S. C.

Marse Didn't Want To See Us Patchety Up

Before the war for freedom, most of our people were treated right at Brookgreen Plantation. Marse Josh Ward and Missus Bess treated us good. Every year when Marse and Missus go to North Carolina mountains, Broad River section, they tell overseer Hemingway, "Don't treat them anyway severe. Don't beat them." But Hemingway was severe. You see, rice was money in that day and time, and there was plenty rice at Brookgreen Plantation.

Pappy liked liquor. Sometimes he would take some rice to town and sell it and buy liquor with the money. One day he came home from town with a jug of whiskey, and the overseer met him at the dock. Pappy dropped the jug and it broke in pieces, but the overseer picked up the pieces. When the day came to go to the barn and pick up rations, no rations were there for Pappy. Instead of putting rations in Pappy's bin, the overseer put pieces of the whiskey jug there to remind Pappy that he had stolen rice and bought whiskey. After that we got our weekly rations of a peck of grits and a half bushel of fine rice. If anybody stole rice, Missus said, "Let them have rice. It is my rice and they are my people. They can have what they need." Most everybody worked in rice.

Everybody except chillun had a task. If you were cleaning, mashing, and leveling the ground where the rice would be planted, your task was a half or a quarter of an acre a day, depending on how old you were. You had to chop the big sods and mash the ground, then fill up the holes and level the whole field. After that, you dug trenches where the rice seed would be planted and you sowed the seeds in the trench. Old Marse Joshua John Ward was king of the rice planters. He owned 1,092 Africans, and his fields yielded nearly four million pounds of rice a year.

Every Sunday morning every gal and boy dress up and go to the yard and Missus Bess gave us candy. We got good clothes. Missus got this blue drilling, yard after yard of that. She had a man name of Thomas Rutledge who was a tailor. He made my little pants. And if you were a gal, he made dress out of same cloth. Marse didn't want to see us patchety up, nor naked. Marse treated us right.

Marse kept three nets running [to supply fish to the plantation]. He sent a man to kill a cow and a hog. He saw that we had a garden. Talk about a garden! Everybody came to see the Brookgreen garden. And orange, and every fruit. Pappy would dig up a ditch pipe and melt it down and make shot for to kill duck. Mammy knew how to cook duck all right. Pappy and his brothers were musicians—Define, Summer, and Daniel Horry. They went all around when the plantation owners had a ball and such as that. Pappy and his brothers were good musicians. One played fiddle; another played fife; the other played drum. Oh, how them white folk's feet did tickle the floor when the Horry brothers played for dancing. I looked in the window and watched them dance.

Before the Yankees came we buried all Missus's good silver and stuff like that right in the garden. Right in Brookgreen garden. Boat carried the Wards to Marlboro County where they would be safe. I remember when the Yankees came. A Yankee boat came and two Yankees got off the boat and our soldiers caught them and they hanged them at the seashore. When the Yankees on the boat found out, oh my Lord! A stir been. What a stir been here. Yankees shelled all the way to Sandy Island. A shell knocked a hole through the sick house at Brookgreen. That place was kept for sick Africans and they got good medical treatment there. After freedom came, we African people dug up everything we had buried in the garden.

BEN HORRY
BROOKGREEN PLANTATION
MURRELLS INLET, S. C.

Isaiah Moore, The Little Storyteller

I was born on Marse John S. Douglas's plantation, close to Little River. When I was birthed, Marse set the name down in a book beside the name of my pappy, Joe, and my mammy, Rachel. Bless the Lord! They belonged to the same Marse and lived on the same plantation, in a teeny log house. The roof leaked and we had a time when it rained. Missus Maggie was a fine woman. She came from the Boyce stock of buckra. She was good to me. We had a white overseer, Mr. Erwin, and if it hadn't been for Missus, I 'spect he'd worn the hide off me one time when he caught me in the watermelon patch. I hoed cotton, picked cotton and peas, and kept the calf off at milking time.

We had to get a pass to go across the plantation property line or we got a whipping and were sent home. Marse had two plantations. One was the home place and the other was the river place, where the corn, oats, and hay were raised. He had a flock of sheep too. All our clothes were made from wool and cotton that was made right there on the plantation. Wool was sheared from the sheep. Cotton was picked from the field. The cotton was hand-carded, then taken to the spinning wheels and made into thread, loomed into cloth, and sewed into clothes or knitted into socks and stockings. Marse had an apparatus to get the seed out of the cotton and packed the lint into bales.

Marse and Missus went to New Hope Church and when I went with them I sat up in the gallery. There was no piano or organ in the church. I looked down at Marse Robin Stinson a many a time and watched him knock a fork on the bench and hold it to his ear to listen to the tune. Then he pitched the tune and all joined in, and let me tell you it had to be one of the Bible psalms instead of a common glory hallelujah hymn.

No sir, Marse and Missus didn't tolerate any African chillun engaging in breaking the Sabbath. In the summertime, after the crops were laid by, we went to hear one of our color expound on the Word in a brush arbor. The preacher was Alfred Moore, the pappy of Isaiah and Phillip Moore. The Reverend searched the scriptures for names for his chillun, Isaiah and Phillip.

Isaiah, one of the preacher's chillun, was a little storyteller and he told a tale about Nicodemus, and all the people in the big house and in the quarters wanted to hear that story. Isaiah allowed that in the days of the disciples there was a small colored man named Nicodemus that ran an eating house in Jerusalem. He did his own cooking and serving at the tables. One day he heard the tramp, tramp, tramp of the multitude coming, and he asked, "What's going on?" He was told that the disciples had borrowed a colt and were having a parade in the city. Nicodemus thought about that and he believed the good Lord Jesus could cure him of the lumbago in his back. Hearing folks shouting, he threw down his dishrag, jerked off his apron, and ran for to see all what was going on, but having short legs, he couldn't see nothing. A big sycamore tree stood in the line of the parade, so Nicodemus climbed up it, going high enough for to see everything. The Savior saw him in the tree and said, "Come down, Nicodemus. We're going to eat at your house." Nicodemus came down so fast that he scraped the bark off the tree in many places. The Savior cured him of the lumbago, but sycamore trees have been blistered ever since.

When the Yankees came they burned down the gin house, took the mules, horses, chickens, and eggs. Marse had been sharp enough to bury the meat in the woods along with other things. After the Yankees set the house afire, they rode off. We put the fire out and saved the mansion for Marse John. I was glad 'cause I wanted to be a friend of Isaiah Moore and listen to his stories. Talk about storytelling!

GEORGE MCALILLEY
LITTLE RIVER, S. C.

Isaiah Moore, The Preacher

NOTE: This is the same Isaiah Moore who was a child in the previous story.

My pappy was Isaiah Moore, and he was the Uncle Remus of all the chillun on the place. He told tales when he was a child during the time when Marse John Douglas was the master of the plantation. Marse Tommie was the master by the time I came along, and Pappy was no longer a child, but a preacher and a storyteller. Many people remembered him from the time when he was a little storyteller.

When I remember Pappy, after he was a grown man, he was still telling the tales, and his sides were shaking and he was laughing. He told all us chilllun the tales about the fox and the rabbit, the squirrel, brer terrapin, and such like, long before Joel Chandler Harris wrote them in a book. He sure did! My mammy's name was Nancy. Nancy and Isaiah Moore, my mammy and pappy, had a baker's dozen. Yes, thirteen head of chillun. Pappy knew all the Bible tales. He could answer every question in the catechism. [Note: Charity Moore kept her father's copy of the catechism, published and dated 1840.]

Pappy still told the story of Adam and Eve and allowed how the devil took the shape of a serpent and glided after Eve. "Somebody's got something for to tell you that will make Adam glad," the serpent said. "Keep your ears open all day long." Then the serpent skeedaddled to the red apple tree, close by the fountain. He beat Eve there because she was walking sorta slow. "Good morning. It's a lovely day. And that is a beautiful apple, just in your reach, too. . . . Just get Adam to eat one bite out of that apple above your head." "Adam is not allowed to eat of the fruit of the tree," said Eve. But the apple looked so good, she reached up, pulled it from the tree, and took a bite. Then she ran to Adam with the rest of it and said, "Husband, eat quick." While he was eating it, and taking the last swallow of the apple, he was reminded of his disobedience and choked twice. Ever since then, a man has an Adam's apple to remind him of the sin of disobedience.

Pappy got old and feeble and Marse Tommie took good care of him when he couldn't work. Even when he wasn't worth much at all, Pappy preached in the pulpit and was a storyteller. When he came to his last days and knew he would soon die, Marse Tommie said, "Is there anything I can do for you, Uncle Isaiah?" "Yes," said Pappy. "I want a white stone over the head of my grave." "What must I put on the stone?" asked Marse Tommie? "Just my name and age," said Pappy. "Oh, there ought to be something else," insisted Marse Tommie. "What else do you want on your stone?" Pappy raised up on an elbow and with a tear and a smile said, "Just put my name and age and under that say 'As good a man as ever fluttered.'" And that stone at Concord Cemetery attracted more attention than any stone and epitaph in the churchyard. I wonder sometime in the winter nights, when the north wind blows, if Pappy is warm and in Abraham's bosom. But I know Pappy. There were so many white folks in his bosom that he'll just be content to lie in peace, or maybe he's in the prophet Isaiah's, for whom he was named.

CHARITY MOORE

They Said I Was Worth $400

My pappy was named Bob and my mammy was named Salina. They belonged to Marse Tom Starke before Marse Nick Peay bought them. My brothers were Bob and John, and I had a sister named Carrie. I was the youngest child. Marse Nick had nineteen plantations, with an overseer and African quarters on every place. Altogether, he owned 27,000 acres which were worked by a thousand Africans, more or less, too many to take a census of. Before the numerator could get around, some more would be born or bought and some would die.

Missus believed there were two classes of folks: the Africans and the poor white folks that didn't own any land. She had a grand manner with the Africans; no patience with poor white folks. They couldn't come in the front yard, and they knew to pass on by and hitch up their horse and come knock on the kitchen door and make their wants and wishes known to the butler.

There were classes among the Africans. The first class were the house Africans that included the butler, maids, nurses, chambermaids, and the cooks. The second class consisted of the carriage drivers, gardeners and carpenters, the barber, and the stableman. Then came the wheelwright, wagoners, blacksmiths, and foremen. The next class were the men who minded the cows and dogs. All had good houses and never had to work hard. They never got a beating. Then came the cradlers of the wheat, the threshers and the millers of the corn and the wheat, and the feeders of cotton to the gin. The lowest class was the field man.

Marse Nick died the year before the war for freedom, and my family left the home place and went to Melrose Plantation, where Marse Nick, Jr. was the master. And what a place that was! 'Twas on a hill, overlooking a fish pond. A flower yard stretched clear down the hill to the big gate, hanging on granite pillars. On the east side of the mansion were the gardens and terraces, acres of sweet potatoes, watermelons, strawberries, and two long rows of beehives.

The house had thirty rooms, 365 windows and doors, one for every day of the year, and the entire house was filled with Marseilles carpets. Linen tablecloths were spread in the dining room where everything was silver, including four wine decanters, four nut crackers, coffee pots, castors for salt and pepper, and silver vinegar bottles. If one counted, there were ninety-eight silver forks, knives, teaspoons and tablespoons, four silver ladles, six silver sugar tongs, silver goblets, a silver mustard pot, and two silver fruit stands. There were silver candlesticks in every room. All fireplaces had brass firedogs and marble mantelpieces. Paintings were of oil, and they hung in the hall. Marse Nick said he paid $100 for each painting. They were of his mammy, pappy, and Uncle Austin and Colonel Lamar.

The smokehouse had four rooms and a cellar. One room every year was filled with brown sugar, just shoveled in with spades. In winter they would drive up a drove of hogs from each plantation, kill them, scald the hair off them, and pack the meat away in salt. They hung up the hams and shoulders in the smokehouse. Most of the rum and wine was kept in barrels in the cellar, but there was a closet in the house where brandy was kept for quick use.

When Marse died, the appraisers for the state came and figured that his enslaved Africans, mules, cows, hogs and things were worth $288,168.78. The land and house were worth over a million dollars. They put a price of $1,800.00 on my mammy and $1,800.00 on my pappy. They said I was worth $400.00. When the Yankees came they loaded up all the meat, took some of the sugar and shoveled some over the yard. They took all the wine, rum, and liquor and took away all the silver and other valuables in the house. Then they set the house afire. They left the Marse and his family in a misery way, and I wept when I saw them so poor. Africans were cold and hungry, but free.

ROSE STARKE
MELROSE PLANTATION
FAIRFIELD COUNTY, S. C.

Owls Hollered Right Regular

I heard owls holler right regular on the plantation. I heard them holler plenty times out there somewhere in the trees. Some of the people who heard them holler stuck a fire iron in the fire and that made the owl quit off. I heard talk about a lot of people who did that.

Then there was another sign the people did on New Years Day. I don't understand much about it, but I did hear people speak about craving a cup of peas and a hunk of hog jowl on the first day of the year. They put their faith in that kind of victuals on New Years Day, and they didn't suffer for anything until that time the next year. I ate my cup of peas and hunk of hog jowl every New Years Day just because I loved it, and I reckon I never gave a thought to that sign.

JESSIE SPARROW
GALIVANTS FERRY, S. C.

Christmas Eve On The Plantation

I went in the big house and the Marse and Missus and all the other people were having a howling time. The big house was all decorated and shining and straining with all the company that come. And the sideboard was so full of victuals it gave a sigh. The smell of that turkey! That ham! That pie! And the snow-white cake piled up with the red berries made my eye sore from looking. My stomach ached for the taste of those things.

I knew that when dark came over everything the big fire would be lighted and the dancing would start and those who could sing would stretch their voices most to Heaven. And I knew that Heaven would just come right down to me. After the people were full of victuals the music started, and my own feet just tickled the floor.

Finally I went home to my mammy, and her face was buried in her apron. I never saw her do that before and she scared me. I said, "Mammy, don't you cry; we got we two, and I done told God to bring us some potato and gravy."

Just then someone knock on the door. I cracked it and saw Missus. She brought us a basket. She come in and open the basket, and that basket ached just thinking about the load that was in it. My eyes lighted on ham! turkey! snow-white cake! Heaven had come right down to me and Mammy on that Christmas Eve.

OPHELIA JEMISON
CHARLESTON COUNTY, S. C.

Everything Passes Over

Marse's name was Jerry Moss, and we lived in Yorkville. My pappy was Henry Rice and my mammy was Charity Rice. Stories were going 'round 'bout Sherman shooting a big rock off the State House in Columbia. Scared of Sherman! And then Sherman came through Yorkville. Things passed over quicker than I figured that they would. Everything, no matter how good or how hard, passes over. Sherman and the Yankees went on somewhere else, I never knew where, and everyone around Yorkville was powerful relieved.

After Sherman went through, Marse and Missus never had anything. Everybody's belly was aching and growling for victuals. I lived on ash cake and 'simmon beer. If locust had been handy, we'd of had locust beer. Every kind of seed and pod that grew we saved for the next spring planting. That year the season was good and the gardens did well. We had worked and waited with nothing in our bellies, and that crop sure was good. We said we would never throw no rations and victuals away again. We took heed and never grumbled 'bout nothing else either.

And then we heard that the Yankees had won the war and our folks had surrendered. I'll never forget seeing them soldiers of ours coming across the river, all dirty, filthy, and lousy. Most starved and poor and lanky. And their horses in the same fix. One soldier fell down in the road, and two buzzards was setting on his shirt when he said, "You is too soon." He grabbed one by the leg and wrung his head off. And then he went home. The women folks took care of the soldiers. They brewed tea from sage leaves, sassafras root, and other herbs. Nobody had money to fetch liniments and salves with.

After the former enslaved men became healthy again they made lots of rail fences. Folks had a no-fence law, that meant everybody fenced in their fields and let the stock run free. Hogs got wild and turkeys were already wild. Sometimes bulls had to be shot to keep them from tearing up everything. The rail fences around the fields were never bigger than ten or fifteen acres. Logs were plentiful, and the men were called rail splitters. That was a good time. We were free, and the men got wages for their work.

JESSIE RICE
YORKVILLE, S. C.

When I Was Eight Years Old
I Started Out In The Field

The big plantation and house what Marse Jimmie Jeter owned is where I first saw earthly light. From a wee bitty baby they taught me to serve. Before you serve God you have got to know how to serve man. We Africans served Him better than the white folks did. Some of the white chillun were real biggity. I did what all little African boys did-sleep and play with the white boys. Lots of playmates, both white and black. Some of the boys I played with saw it powerful hard, living like we did. Others never saw it so bad. It depends on you a lot and it depends on them that you stayed with. When I was eight years old I started out in the field.

When war raged all 'round Charleston and Columbia, Yankees camped a half mile from Santuc. Everybody was scared. When them Yankees got to Santuc, Mammy was weaving just as hard as she could for her Missus. She started to run, but the Yankees came into the house and took her yarn and pulled her into the yard. They tied her to a tree and stomped the yarn in the dirt. The Yankees never burned anything in the house, though, and Mammy got the yarn up from the dirt, cleaned it, and went back to work. The Yankees didn't stay in Santuc very long.

BOB YOUNG
JETER PLANTATION
SANTUC, S. C.

My Young Missus Gave Me A Test

My Marse was Jesse Kilgo, and my Missus was Letha Kilgo. When their daughter named Catherine married Marse Watt Wardlaw, I was given to Missus Catherine for a housemaid, 'cause I was trim and neat. Young Missus Catherine said, "Delia, come to my room. I'm going to give you a test to see if I can put up with you." I went to that room, in the wintertime mind you, and Missus Catherine cocked one of her pretty feet on the firedog. Some folks call them andirons, but I call them firedogs. She said, "Delia, put kettle water on the fire." So I did that in a jiffy. Her next command was, "Would you please be so kind as to sweep and tidy up the room?" All the time turning that lovely head of hers like a bird a-building a nest. I did that, and then she said, "You are going to make a maid, and a good one." She gave a silvery giggle and said, "I just had you put on that water for to see if you were going to make any water slop out of the pan. No! You didn't spill a drop; you are not going to be a sloppy maid. You are just fine." Then she called her mother in. "See how pretty Delia made this room? Look at the curtains, drawn back just right. Observe the pitcher and the towels on the washstand. I'm proud of her." She gave old Missus a hug and a kiss, and thanked her for me as a wedding present.

Did we get any religion told to us? Well, it was this way: Missus talked a heap to us 'bout the Lord, but Marse talked a heap to us 'bout the devil. 'Twixt and 'tween them, I 'spect we heard most everything 'bout Heaven and the devil.

The Yankees came, yes they did. But they were gentlemen. They never took a thing, but left provisions for our women folks from their commissary.

DELIA THOMPSON
LIBERTY HILL, S. C.

Ole Man Chisolm Blew His Horn At Dayclean

Pappy belonged to General Butler; my mammy was a Maner, but originally she was drawn out of the Robert estate. The Roberts were wealthy folks. Bill Robert had so much money that he said he was going to the end of the world. He came back and said he went so close to hell that the heat drew the pitch from his vessel. He lost his eyesight by it. It wasn't long before he was stone blind.

The enslaved Africans were waked up every morning by the driver blowing a horn. Ole Man Jack Chisolm was his name. Just at dayclean he'd put his horn through a crack in the upper part of the wall to his house and blow it through that crack. Then the under-driver would go out and round them up. After they did their day work, they came home, washed up, and cooked their supper. Then Ole Man Jake Chisolm blew his horn to let them know it was time to go to bed. Sometimes in my pappy's cabin, he had to put out the fire and finish eating supper in the dark.

If you wanted to send any news to anybody on another planta-tion, the overseer would write the message for you and send it by a boy to the overseer of the other plantation, and he'd read it to the one you wrote it to.

PHOEBE FAWCETTE
HAMPTON COUNTY, S. C

We Got Our Freedom On Sunday.

Parson Glennie, rector of All Saints church, came to Sunnyside once a month. Told us to obey Missus. Parson Glennie went to every plantation once a month. He musta liked to preach at Hagley Plantation 'cause Marse Weston built beautiful St. Mary's chapel from materials what came from England. Marble baptismal font and stained glass windows. No such chapel at Sunnyside, 'cause that was a big ole summer house on the creek at Murrells Inlet. But we listened to Parson Glennie.

All enslaved people were taught in the faith of their marses—the Episcopal. Sometimes when Dr. Glennie wasn't there, we'd fight. She knocked me. I knocked back. Wouldn't take a knock. She'd say, "I'll tell Parson Glennie, and the Lord won't bless you. You're bad." I say, "You knock me, I knock you!" When Parson Glennie didn't come, Missus taught us. Baked big ole cake and served after the catechism. We played play-house and marbles, and at night we went to prayer meeting.

Four years of the war we'd been holding prayer meetings. Praying for freedom. We had prayer meeting many a time 'til the chicken crowed for day. Everybody wanted freedom. Prayed for it. And then we heard that the Yankees were coming. We heard that the Yankees were killing horses and throwing them in the wells to pollute the water. I wanted to protect from Yankees, to hide. On the day they came, I didn't hide. Was standing in the house. It was on a Sunday.

You could hear the Yankees slamming, banging, and tearing up everything. Big guns shooting! The big house, Sunnyside, was jarred. Water shake out of the glass. Sunnyside was one of the dignified homes built by the Alstons. Big oak trees in yard. Sea-beach beyond the sand dunes. The Yankees came in gunboats. I went outside with Missus Susan Alston. She took her spyglass and stood behind one of the big trees and spied them big boats shooting! Marse say, "Don't get in front of tree—they might shoot you." Old African people gathered in the yard. They said, "Thank God!" "Marse, he's coming. Freedom's *coming!*"

"What's coming, Grandma?" a child asked.

"You'll know. You all will know!"

The Yankees came and told Marse no more slave holding. He told his people we were free. All the African men took their master's title. Joe became Joe Belin as he was Parson Belin's man. Fred had already taken the name of Poinsette from another marse. All the right-hand servant took their marse's title.

I know when Lincoln shoot the chain of slavery off my neck.

MARIAH HEYWOOD
MURRELLS INLET, S. C.

Been To The Devil And Come Back

I lived on the Ark plantation, in upper All Saints Parish. When I was very small I would run to marse and ask for sugar. Marse'd say, "What you crying for?" Missus Martha would say, "He's crying for you to give him some sugar." "Bring the boy here, Martha." Marse always gave me sugar. Plenty sugar, but we had to make salt at the sea-beach.

Marse had a platform over the sea water, like a wharf. A pump was on the platform, and I used to pump the brine up to the vats. The sun and the wind caused the water in the brine to evaporate, leaving salt behind. I toted salt to the big house in containers of cedar and cypress. My grandmammy didn't make her salt that way. She boiled the brine. Boiled all day and all night. Stirred the pot with cedar paddle.

My mammy made ash cake with meal, salt, and water. No grease. I saw her cook it many a hundred days. We had plenty to eat, corn, meat, pig, beef, fish, heap of milk. When a cow wouldn't give much milk, it was called a "coffee cow." That meant it gave only enough milk for coffee.

Marse made a fortune on indigo. Planted indigo like corn. The field hands used oxen to pull the plows in the fields. Seed was like flax seed. We put myrtle seed in with indigo to boil and make a purple dye, which was sold to people in England. The chillun in the quarters wore caprous pants. They were dyed purple out of a homemade dye, which if gotten wet or perspired on would run. Once a boy put on a pair, and when he perspired the color faded and dyed his skin. He thought he was in the throes of death and he ran home frightened and said he thought he was mortifying.

When rice came into circulation, Marse did away with indigo. He made bigger fortune from rice. Women worked in rice. Had to plant seed in March. Brought in sea water on incoming tide and flowed over the fields. Harvested in late summer.

Had a sick house and a chillun house. All the chillun stay in chillun house while mammies worked in the fields. Women too old to work in the fields took care of them.

Ole Man John Tilghman was the driver. He treated his people good, but a man couldn't marry without the consent of the overseer.

I remember when 'mancipation came. Freedom came and was like having been to the Devil and come back.

SABE RUTLEDGE
THE ARK PLANTATION
HORRY COUNTY, S. C.

Great-grandmammy Was Captured By A Pirate

During the English war [Revolutionary War], my great-grandmammy, Veenia, who was a little child, was traveling with her Missus who was trying to escape England and come to the Ark Plantation in South Carolina. In that day and time, ladies wore a gold chain on which a little bag containing a needle, thimble and thread was attached. Such a gold chain was fastened to the shoulder of the Missus's dress.

While the Missus and the child Veenia were on a ship that had departed from New York and was bound for South Carolina, pirates overtook the vessel and began taking anything of value from the passengers. A man with the skull and crossbones on his hat went straight for the Missus and yanked off the gold chain with needle, thimble and thread. Little Vennia ran to Missus and twisted herself in Missus's long skirt. The buccaneer noticed that they were together and he let it be. He put her and Veenia off at Wilmington. They had a very rough time of trying to get to South Carolina and finally made their way to Pitch Landing, on the Waccamaw River. Someone told them where the Ark Plantation was, and they arrived there one day.

That's the way my family came to South Carolina. My great-grandmammy Veenia lived to the age of 110, and although she didn't have a tooth in her head she could eat hard bread as good as anybody.

SABE RUTLEDGE
THE ARK PLANTATION

The Yankees Tied Me Up By My Thumbs

When the Yankees came they tied me up by my two thumbs and tried to make me tell where I had hid the money, the gold watch, and the silver. I said I didn't know. Oh, yes, I knew where it was. I had hid it two years before.

The Yankees left and we were free, but we didn't know 'cause Marse Brice never said a word to us. I was free three years before I knew about it. One day we were in the field and a man came along on a big, black horse, its tail plaited and tied with a red ribbon. He waved his hands and shouted, "You is free, all of you. Go anywhere you want to." That's the first I knew that I was free. We just worked, same as before freedom. We got meat, hominy, and cornmeal on Mondays and wheat bread, lard, and 'lasses on Saturdays.

One day Marse Brice told me to go to the woods and find the money, the gold watch, and the silver. I went to the woods and searched, but I couldn't find it. I remembered that I had spaded the dirt by a pine stump, put the keg in and covered it up with leaves and left it. Marse looked like he thought I was a liar and a thief. Then one day I was riding in a cart pulled by a mule, and as the mule's foot sank down into the old stump hole I saw the keg with the money, the gold watch and the silver. Marse was mighty glad that I was not a liar and a thief.

ANDY MARION
UPPER SOUTH CAROLINA

Manners Will Carry People Through Anything

I belonged to Marse Giles Evanson and lived at the place called Ash Pole Plantation. Marse owned my mother and eight head of her chillun. He never had nothing but women people. Marse said he didn't want no men on the plantation. I was the house girl and worked for the Missus, washing her chillun's hair and putting them to bed.

Missus never wore no cotton clothes. She had her silk on every day and them long yellow earbobs that touched her shoulder. She wore wool in the winter. Had lots of sheep, which they sheared in May. Made all kind of nice cloth then, and blankets. I was a little girl when the Yankees came through. They looked just like a big blue cloud a-coming down that road. We chillun scared of them.

Marse and Missus never wanted me to marry, but when I was about sixteen, I married and had a nice wedding, right there in Marse's yard. Wore white dress. Marse and Missus were against it, but they never said nothing. They had good manners. Manners will carry people through anything.

NANCY WASHINGTON
MARION, S. C.

We Played Games Like Marbles And Anti-Over

I was a boy on Marse Pierce Lake's plantation, and I worked and piddled around the house. Sometimes I had to hoe the corn in the garden. Marse had a big garden. My sister worked in the big house, and she learned to read and write. They never taught me to read and write. We chillun played games like marbles and anti-over. To play anti-over a crowd of chillun get on each side of the house and someone throws a ball from one side to the other. Whoever gets the ball runs around to the other side and touches somebody with it, and that person is out of the game. One of the dances was "Jump Jim Crow." A boy or girl would jump up and down while tripping and dancing in the same spot. We had what we called a Juber game. "Juber this. Juber that. Juber killed a yellow cat."

Some of the folks had remedies for curing, like making hot tea from a weed called boneset. That weed grows wild in the woods. The teas were bitter, but it was good for chills and fever. Little bags of asafetida were hung around the chillun's neck to ward off fever or diphtheria.

We called the cows on the plantation like this: "Co-winch, cowinch." We called the mules like this: "Co, co." And the hogs and pigs: "Pig-oo, pig-oo."

Marse gave us three days off at Christmas. Had plenty good things to eat. Marse gave all us chillun little pieces of candy.

JOHN DAVENPORT
CHAPIN, S. C.

A Nice Set Of People

Marse took me as a little boy as a pet. A little bed was right by his bed in the big house, and he put me in the little bed. Every morning they brought Marse his breakfast tray, and I ate off that tray. Marse kept two of his finest horses for his carriage, and he took me with him in the carriage.

I fared well, 'cause I was Marse's pet, but old man Aldridge was a mean overseer. Some found it powerful hard working for Aldridge. They planted cotton, corn, peas, potatoes, and all the time Aldridge would lick them.

Old man Aldridge is gone now, but there can't be no rest for him. Oh, no! He treated them so mean and finally I told Marse about it, and when Marse heard it he discharged him. Then Marse got Chisolm. After Chisolm came, everything was just as sweet and smooth as could be. The Chisolms were a nice set of people.

SAM TRUE
GREENVILLE, S. C.

Mammy Was Bitten By A Rattlesnake

It required more than 1,000 enslaved Africans to work old Marse Josh Ward's fields on the Waccamaw. Marse Josh was one of the largest owner of Africans in the nation. In 1850 he produced 'bout four million pounds of rice. My mammy worked in rice for Marse Josh. She wore no shoes and used her ankles to bank up the dirt around the plants. Her ankles were about as hard as a rock.

One day when Mammy was working with her heels, a rattlesnake went into his coil and sounded his bells. You know they always give warning before they bite. Well that ole serpent sank its fangs in Mammy's ankle. She tried to shake it off, but the snake was too long and too heavy. She looked this way, and that, but nobody was there to help her.

She lit out home, hollering, and trying to drag that monster what was hanging on for its life. When Mammy got home, I saw what the trouble ws and called Pappy. He tried to yank it off her heel, but it wouldn't budge. Finally, Pappy cut off part of Mammy's heel. I grieved and cried that night, and Pappy told me that Mammy was well. The snake's fangs had lodged in the callous on her heel, and none of the venom had gotten in her blood. He laughed 'bout that, but I didn't laugh. Mammy had to pull that rattlesnake home on her heel, running like she had the rheumatism.

JOHN
MURRELLS INLET, S. C.

I Was Scared Half To Death Of Stocking Foot

We lived in a one-room log cabin with a stick chimney. One time, in cold wintertime with the wind a-blowing, the stick got afire and burned a big hole in the back of the chimney. The house was full of fire-sparks, ashes and smoke, but we lived there for two weeks before they built another chimney just like the old one.

There were so many Africans on Marse's plantation that you couldn't count them. One day Marse sold one of Mammy's chillun, and she carried on so about it Marse said, "Stop that sniffing if you don't want to get a whipping." She cried all night about it.

Marse was a rich man. Before Christmas he would kill thirty hogs and after Christmas, thirty more. He had a big gin house and sheep, goats, cows, mules, horses, turkeys, geese, and a stallion named Stocking Foot. We little chillun were scared to death of Stocking Foot. Mammy made me be good by saying, "Better hush, Stocking Foot will get you and tramp you down." I got real quiet after that.

We looked for the coming of the Yankees on that place the same as we looked for the Savior and host of angels at the second coming. The Yankees came one day in February. They took everything off the plantation and burned the big house, stables, barn, and gin house, but they left the cabins in the quarters. The song of Moses came into my mind: The Lord had triumphed glorily and the horse and his rider had been thrown into the sea

SUE BURRELL
COLUMBIA, S. C.

The Escape Of Tom Wells

One of the little chillun came running over to our cabin to tell Pappy something: "Tom Wells is trying to kill Marse with an axe and Marse says to come quick!" Pappy and I went running to the other yard and saw Marse and Tom struggling to get control of the axe. Pappy separated them and made Tom drop the axe. Tom turned to Pappy and said, "I 'spect I better light out, 'cause it will be a bleeding back for me, if not death, if I stay on this plantation." And then Tom Wells struck out, too angry to say another word, and he ran all the way to Newberry.

Freedom came to the plantation, and nobody knew where Tom was. Finally Tom came back, and this is what he said: "I had been praying for freedom, and worrying over my burdens of bonds. That morning Marse cussed me awful and said he was going to whup me 'til my back ran blood. I grabbed the axe and waded in, not knowing which one of us would die. Marse was strong. And then a man came and shamed both of us.

"I ran until I came to some cabins and the people there fed me. At night I lay in the woods, half asleep and listening for Marse and his bloodhounds. As I got stronger, I traveled all night and lay around in the day. After I reached the big mountains, I got along better; people seemed less 'spicious and kinder.

"I kept going until I reached Kentucky and found a woman by the name of Tubbs. She had a black face but a white heart, and she had seventeen runaways in charge. She told me to be ready the next day to ride the underground railroad to freedom.

"The next morning we walked fully a mile underground until we reached a little train. Some were already on board, and the train was crowded when we left for freedom. Food was on the train, a sack of meat, bread, and two gallons of water.

"In a day or two we got off and walked up big steps and there was the world again. Some white men and women helped us find food and work. After that I soon had money and a wife. We prospered but the wife and two chillun died. I came back to my old stamping ground. I like the climate better."

WILLIAM HOUSSAL
NEWBERRY, S. C.

The Boy Who Sold Himself For $20

I was born on February 24, 1852, on a plantation one and a half miles from Mars Bluff. The big house was built high off the ground, and I drove carts under that house lots of times. Houses in the quarters were small. The people in the quarters slept on bunk beds that had four legs and mattress of shucks or cotton. Boy chillun had shucks bed and the girl chillun had cotton bed.

I wore homemade clothes. My mammy spinned and loomed and dyed my clothes. Sometimes she made the dye out of persimmon juice, but if I wanted something a different color she would use something else. Mammy made hoe cake, and I liked it best of all. She mixed up the cake and put it on the hoe and set the hoe in the ashes until the hoecake was cooked. She saw to it that I had a Sunday suit, made out of cotton, and my shoes were leather, made on the plantation.

Missus Lizzie, a daughter of Marse Colonel William Wilson, carried some of us chillun to church at Hopewell, down below Claussens. I recollect Missus Lizzie told me one Sunday that if I didn't change my chat she would whip me. "You go up in the gallery with the other chillun, and if you don't behave yourself I'm going to whip you on Monday," she said. They taught us the catechism, and she asked me, "Charles, who made you?" I said, "Pappy made me." "Who made you?" she insisted. "Pappy made me." I sure thought that was so. She took the Bible and told me that God made me.

I went home and told Pappy Missus Lizzie said she was going to beat me Monday morning for saying he made me. Pappy told me that Missus Lizzie was right: God made me. I changed my chat and saved my beating.

One day a man from North Carolina visited Marse, and Marse wanted to give him some entertainment. Marse called me and said he had a bear in a cage and wanted me to go into the cage and fight the bear. I didn't want to do it, but Marse kept on. He unlocked the door and shoved me in and locked the door so I couldn't get out.

Right at that moment I realized a rattlesnake also was in the cage. A lot of other people gathered around to watch me fight the bear. Marse said, "Gentlemen you're going to see a boy fight a bear." Then he said to me, "You have to fight the bear now." I screamed, "Great God, get me out of here." Marse dashed some sweet water on my head and the bear went for my head. He scratched me a little bit, but he lapped up the sweet water. The bear turned around and didn't seem to want to fight. Marse said, "The bear didn't hurt him, but the rattlesnake will kill him."

Dr. Poston stepped out from the crowd and said, "Let the boy out and give him some medicine." Marse let me out, paid me $1.50 and gave me two bottles of medicine.

When I thought about how cruel Marse was, I ran away to Charleston and sold myself. I went to the Custom House and told them I wanted to sell myself for $20. Someone asked me for how long I was selling myself, and I said for four years. They asked me what kind of job I wanted. I told them most anything. They said, "Well, there is a vessel out there waiting for some hands." The vessel was better than 100 feet long. The mate's name was Charlie and he helped me.

We went to Liberia and then to Africa. Had to sail around a whale and then an iceberg. In four years we came into port at Georgetown. I had never been paid the $20 for which I had sold myself.

CHARLIE GRANT
FLORENCE, S. C.

The Ball Gown

One day the Missus appraised me keenly and said I had just shot up in height. Family forms and features run pretty true to patterns and, like my mammy, I was tall, but I had a little bitty wasp-like waist and tiny wrists. Missus said for me to come into the big house as she wanted her seamsters to fit a ball dress on me. The material made my eyes bug out. It was the finest mull with flowered panels running through it. The seamsters threw the material around me this way and that and draped it over my shoulders. Hoops were placed from the shoulders to the elbows, and the cloth was puffed over the hoops into great sleeves.

When they were finished I went back to the quarters, and several days later Missus summoned me back to the big house. The dress had been hand-sewn in the tiniest fine stitches and had mighty fine cording in the seams. After it had been placed on me just to perfection, a silver mantilla shawl completed the costume. I turned around and around so everyone could view it and see that everything had been done to perfection. I asked the seamsters, who lived in the quarters, who the dress was being made for, and they didn't know.

Several weeks later I saw my Missus on her mare. She reined in her horse and said, "Sarah, I want to thank you for allowing the ball gown to be fitted on you. You are the exact size of the person who wore it to a historic ball. "Yas'm," I answered, "and who might that person be?" "She was my relative," said Missus, "Miss Alicia Snowden of Alabama, and her escort to the second inaugural ball of President Washington was an officer on General Washington's staff. The escort just might become Alicia's husband someday, and the ball gown will have a lot to do with it. He said the gown was one of the finest he had ever laid eyes on.

SARAH BOYLSTON
ALLENDALE, S. C.

Little Ike Went Down Into The Water

When Marse Johnnie married Missus Minnie Mobley, my mammy, my pappy, and I were given to them. We lived in a log house close to the spring, where we got water. Mammy did the Missus's washing every week. I kept the fires burning around the pots so the water would keep boiling. Pappy was a field hand and plowed a big red mule named Esau. All the people who worked in the fields during cotton-picking time sang "Glory Hallelujah" all day long. Each person picked two bales a day. We had good rock chimneys to our house, plank floors, movable bedsteads with wheat straw mattresses, and cotton pillows.

Every Sunday they fetched us to the catechism and told us who made us, what He made us out of, and what He made us for. And they told us that from the crown of our heads to the top of our big toes, the chief end of every finger and even to the ends of our two thumbs, we were made to glorify the Lord! Missus was more 'ticular about the catechism that Marse. Her grandpappy, old Marse John Mobley, was a great Baptist.

After the crops were laid by every August, he visited Missus Minnie, and while there, he dammed up the branch and took all the enslaved Africans there to be baptized. I've seen twenty-seven go down and come up out of that pool, a-splashing water from their faces.

A terrible thing happened one time at the baptism. It was while the war was going on, and Marse Johnnie had come back from Virginia on a furlough for ten days. Old Marse John Mobley came to see him and fetched Reverend Marse Cartledge with him. Everybody was powerful concerned about religion along about that time. I was with all the chillun who were to be baptized by Marse Cartledge.

A little boy named Ike was to be baptized that night. We chillun were dressed in a kind of white slipover gown for the occasion. When it came Ike's time to receive the baptism, he was led by his mammy to the edge of the water, and his hand was given to the preacher, who received him.

About that time Ike broke loose and ran up the bank, and his mammy and everybody hollered "Ketch him! Ketch him!" Ike was caught and fetched back to Marse John, who explained that it was better to have water in the nose than fire in the soul. The preacher put his hand over Ike's eyes and nose and turned him down under that water. The preacher lost his hold and in some way Ike got between the preacher's legs and came up behind him. Ike turned somersaults and ran out on the bank.

Ike's mammy cried out "Ketch him!" Marse said no, just let him go. "We'll just drop him in another time."

BILL WILIAMS
BLACKSTOCK, S. C.

That Was The Saddest Day
Of That Day And Time

We lived in a four-room log house. There were Pappy and Mammy, Grandpapppy Henry, Grandmammy Kisana, Aunt Anna and her seven chillun, and me and my two brothers and two sisters. Well, that is the number piled in there at night in the beds and on the floors. I was just a little fellow, running 'round most of the time in my shirttail, but I picked cotton and piddled around the woodpile, fetching wood for the big house and chips and kindling to fresh up the fires.

We had plenty to eat, because we killed thirty-five hogs at a time, and the sausages were a sight. We made lard, and crackling bread. I was always hungry for crackling bread.

When we went to church the preacher asked us to join in some of the hymns, especially about the fountain filled with blood and the one about amazing grace how sweet the sound that saved a wretch like me. I remember a song the white folks sang one day at a wedding, "Hark From The Tomb A Doleful Sound." Don't you think that was the wrong song to sing on a wedding day? "Joy To The World" was in our hearts and that tune would have been more appropriate, it seems to me.

Marse Charlie went off to the war and got killed at the Second Bull Run. When the Yankees came they made me run after chickens and I had to give up the blue hen that belonged to me. After I gave them my blue hen, that was the saddest day of that day and time.

All the enslaved Africans had to go to Winnsboro and register and get a name. One of Marse's boys was a dwarf, and he said, "Marse, I don't want no little name, I want a big-sounding name." Marse wrote on the paper, then he read, "Your name is Mendozah J. Fernandez, and I hope that's big enough for you." The little dwarf seemed powerful pleased and registered his new name. The rest of us spoke to Marse and he said there was no better name than Woodward, so we took that name. It been a kind of a protection to us, and my family said they would never drag it in a jail. Bless God! I hope none of us ever will.

ALEX WOODWARD
WINNSBORO, S. C.

I Had Visions Of My Mammy

Marse John gave us chillun to his daughter, Missus Marion, and we moved down to the June place. We were separated from our mammy, whose name was Martha. She was a mighty pretty woman and I had visions and dreams of her. My sisters called me Cally, but my mammy never did. She said Caleb every time and all the time.

I was born in the old Bell house on Christmas Eve, 1851, in Blackstock, South Carolina. That's where I first came to light. Most chillun don't know the day or the place where they were born. Had to take that on faith.

There were a whole passel of Africans in the quarters, three hundred or maybe more. I didn't count them 'cause I couldn't count more than a hundred, but I could count a hundred. Ten, ten, double ten, forty-five and fifteen. Don't that make a hundred? Sure it does.

There were too many people to have much clothes. I belonged to the shirttail brigade. I used to plow in my shirttail. It wasn't so bad in the summertime.

We had preaching in the quarters on Sunday. Uncle Dick, an old man, was the preacher. The funerals were simple and held at night. The grave was dug that day.

A man who had a wife off the place saw little peace or happiness. He could see the wife once a week, on a pass, and jealousy kept him distracted the balance of the week if he loved her very much.

CALEB CRAIG
BLACKSTOCK, S. C.

I Was Bound To The Blacksmith

I was bound out to Jim Gregory, a blacksmith for Marse Johnny and his wife, Missus Polly. They lived in the Meader House, a brick house built by Missus Polly's father, Triplett Meador. Missus Polly was a little girl when the house was built. While the brick for the drawing room fireplace were still wet, he made little Polly step on each one of them to make the impression of her feet. So those little footprints in that fireplace are Missus Polly's when she was five years old. She grew up there, married, and lived there with Marse Johnny.

Jim Gregory made plows in his blacksmith shop from ten-inch sheet iron. The sheet was heated and beaten into shape with his hammer. After cooling, the tools could be shaped. Horse and mule shoes were made from slender iron rods. They were called "slats," and this grade of iron was known as "slat iron." The shoe was molded while hot, and beaten into the correct shape to fit the animal's feet. Those shoes fit just right. The horseshoe nails were made there. Every farm implement of iron was made from flat or sheet iron.

Mammy sewed the first pants that I wore. She wove and finished them with her hands. She made the thread that they were sewed with by hand. I wore homemade cotton underwear in summer and winter, for we were poor. Of course winter clothes were heavier. Marse raised some sheep, and the winter woolens were made from the wool sheared from the sheep every May. Wool was then made into yarn. Mammy ran it off on spools for her loom.

Missus Polly allowed no patrollers on the place, for she did her own patrolling with her own whip and two bull dogs. She never had an overseer on her place either. Neither did she let anyone else do the whipping, but she did her own. One night she went to the quarters and found old Bill Pea Legs there after he had scared one of the women. She gave old Bill Pea Legs a whipping he never forgot.

Morg used to sit on the meat block every Saturday and cut the meat for Missus Polly to give out. Morg would eat her three pounds of raw meat right there. I asked her what she did the rest of the week without any meat. She said she took the skin and greased her mouth every morning, then went to the field and did her work and waited until the next Saturday for more.

I remember when the Yankees came. I saw Wheeler and his men when they stopped at the gin house. They began to ransack immediately. Wheeler gave some orders and his men galloped off toward our house in the quarters.

All the people in the quarters ran away except Mammy and me. Wheeler rode up in front of the door and spoke to Mammy. He said that he had to feed his men and horses and asked her where the corn was. She told him that the gin house and the crib, which contained the corn did not belong to her, so she could not give him the keys. At that he ordered his men to remove a log from the crib. They broke into the crib and got all the corn.

Then they ransacked the house and took everything there was to eat. They camped in the gin for the night. The next morning they set fire to the gin and then galloped away, taking with them all our corn and the fodder, 200 bundles that we had in the barn.

JOHN BOYD
UNION, S. C.

The Peoples Had to Cook In The Fireplace

The chimneys in the cook house were made ten feet wide and out of wood, which was mortared thick with mud to keep it from catching fire. Skillets and other pots and pans were placed inside for cooking, and some distance above these were hooks for hanging quarters of beef so they would dry thoroughly during the winter. Six-foot logs were placed in the fireplace. I remember all about when the peoples had to cook in the fireplace because that's all that was in circulation for cooking.

Tan Yard Hill was about two miles north of Newberry Courthouse, and that is where we went for tanning.

We picked plenty of cotton. After the cotton was picked, we took the seeds out by hand. A frolic followed that, and we young people had a howling good time. The old people came for the big supper given by Marse.

JAMES CALDWELL
NEWBERRY, S. C.

She Was Mighty Particular About My Manners

Missus Newberry taught me my letters and the Bible, and she was mighty particular about my manners. My manners brought me a heap of blessings. We lived at Airlie Plantation on Middle Sound, and that is where I was born. My mammy cooked for Missus Newberry, and she liked her missus so much she took her name. Mammy was Hattie Newberry.

My, but we had birds and possums on the Sound! Partridges all over the place. Me and Mammy ate partridge for breakfast. And fish! Talk about fish! There were fish in the Sound. One day when I was carrying my fish in to Airlie Plantation Marse Pem heard me laugh. After that, those quality folks liked for me to laugh for them. My mouth is bigger than usual and my voice is deep. Marse Pem gave me a suit of fine clothes and a tall silk hat. That outfit was too big for me, but they liked for me to dress in that long-tail coat and high-top hat and laugh for them and their guests.

One time a Marse Fish was a visitor at the big house. Now that tickled me. I could just laugh and laugh about that name. I'd eat a big dinner in the kitchen where Mammy was, then put on my coat and silk hat and go in amongst the quality and laugh for them and make my noise like a wood saw in my throat. They were crazy about that. I could make that buzzing sound that came from some mysterious depth of my stomach go on for three minutes with no effort. And then's when I began to be thankful about my manners. I have noticed if you have nice manners with everybody, people will be nice to you.

After freedom came, me and Mammy and the Newberrys had all we needed. We never paid no attention to freedom or not freedom. I remember everybody had work to do and they went right on doing it. Nobody didn't get nowhere setting down holding their hands. It don't make much difference anyhow what you do just so you do it.

JOHN EVANS
AIRLIE PLANTATION
WRIGHTSVILLE BEACH, N. C.

Raw Oysters, Roast Oysters, Oyster Stew and Fried Oysters

My name is Daphney Wright, but they called me "Affie." I lived on a plantation on the river, but the summer place was ten miles away, near Bluffton, and that is where I summered with Marse Robert and Missus. But I lived on the plantation except for the four years when we refuged from the Yankees.

That plantation was a beautiful place, there on the water. When the stars would come out over the water it was a beautiful sight. Sometimes some of us chillun would get in a little boat and paddle out into the river. We'd be scared to go too far out, but we'd paddle around. Sometimes Pappy would go out in the night and catch the fish with a seine. He'd come back with a bushel of fish almost anytime. They were nice big mullets. He'd divide them around amongst the people in the quarters and those in the big house. He'd take the fish to the big house before breakfast.

Folks in the big house ate well. Bacon was cut into little pieces and fried into cracklings then put into the fish stew. They ate raw oysters, roast oysters, oyster stew, and fried oysters, and those big crabs and little clams. When the tide would go out, you could just pick up the crabs.

The southern soldiers came through Bluffton on a Wednesday and told us the Yankees were right behind them. The butler buried the silver in a big hurry. Big old teapot, tray, everything buried deep down. Then we all left Bluffton and refuged the first night at Jonesville. From there we went to Hardeeville. We traveled in wagons and buggies. A house was found for us to stay but Marse, Missus, and their chillun went on farther up the country, to a safer place. They went to Society Hill. Stayed four years.

When we all got back to the plantation, the Yankees came through. One said, "I came to set you free. You can stay with your old owners if you wants to, but they'll pay you wages." The Yankees sure did plenty of mischief while they were there. Went through the house and took everything they could find.

The butler was walking down the road after the war, and Wheeler's Brigade killed him. After that, the silver was never found. Nobody knew where the butler had buried it.

You know, after the Confederate War, money was confiscated. You could be a-walking along the road anytime and pick up a ten dollar bill or a five dollar bill, but it wasn't no good to you. After the greenback came, money flourished again.

DAPHNEY WRIGHT
SCOTIA, S. C.

My Great-grandpappy Was Brought Straight From Africa

My great-grandpappy on Pappy's side was brought straight from Africa. The ship was anchored near Sullivans Island, where the Africans were fed like dogs. Peas were cooked in a big pot and set aside to cool. Everybody went to the pot and ate with their hands from the pot.

Things were not that bad on the plantation where we lived. Pappy told me that the plantation and thousand acres were given to Marse by the King of England. We had plenty vegetables all the time in the three-acre garden. Pappy got up early and worked the garden, then he went to the field at 7:00. Provisions were distributed on Monday evenings.

Marse had big places on Big Island and Coals Island in Beaufort County. He didn't have an overseer. Pappy was his driver.

When a young man would call on Marse and say he wanted to marry, Marse would say yes. That night more chicken would be fried and everything eatable would be prepared and Marse would dine the couple. Then the couple went home, without any reading of matrimony of man and wife.

After the war was over, a man I knew picked out a woman he wanted to marry. He didn't know who she was because he was sold when he was about eight years old. They were married about a month, and one night they started to tell of their experiences and the man found out that the woman he had married was his mammy.

HENRY BROWN
BEAUFORT, S. C.

No Marse To Tell Them What To Do

Marse was at the war, and Missus took over. She called all us to sit down on the side steps with our hats in our hands, and she read from the paper. When she got through, we still sat. She waited a few minutes, then she said, "It means that you all are free. Just as free as I am." Dumpling Pie jumped up and started crying. We all looked at him, because he was a fat, lazy thing who lay around like dumplings laying over kraut. We asked him what he was crying for. He said, "I don't want to be free, because that brings in the Issue, and I want to keep my mammy and pappy."

It was the awfulest feeling that everybody in the quarters laid down with that night, the new feeling that they were free and never had no marse to tell them what to do. I felt just like I had done strayed off a-fishing and got lost. The next morning, Missus said, "Silas, I want you to keep on being my houseboy." That sounded the best to me of any news that I had got. A lot of the people in the quarters moved away, but I stayed on with Missus Sallie.

One dark, rainy, cold day a stranger came riding up on a poor horse and fetched a note of sorrow. Marse Dusey had done died somewhere, and Missus was widowed to the ground. Marse's name was John Smith, but it appears like there were so many John Smiths he was called John Dusey.

SILAS SMITH
GAFFNEY, S. C.

Missus Joanna Married a Yankee

Marse Campbell, a Yankee man, married Missus Joanna Perry, whose pappy was Marse Oliver Perry of Bouknights Ferry on the Saluda River. Missus Joanna was married on Friday in the drawing room all fixed up with cedar ropes a-hanging from the ceiling and the most candles what everybody ever did see. She had made us build her an arch and cover it with vines. It set before the mantel and a white bell hung from the middle of it. White cloth was stretched over everything and they never let nobody walk in that room except in their bare feet for fear they would dirty all that cloth.

Missus Isabella picked the piano for Missus Joanna. A lady from another plantation sang two songs. They wore the prettiest white dresses with flowers in their hair. Missus Joanna had her face all covered up with a thin white cloth that fell off her and laid all back over her and to the floor. The bride's maids wore white dresses what laid over the floor but didn't none of them have their faces covered up except Missus Joanna. You see, she was the bride. My mammy, the cook, was rigged in white herself.

Everything in that house was fixed up extra for the ceremony. I was little but I wore a man's black coat and black pants and a white shirt with a vest and tie. The seamsters had made it fit me. I had on a fine pair of black shoes. Marse and Missus gave all that to me and said I could keep it after the wedding.

The next day, Saturday, came the big infair. A double table was set up in the dining room. Ham, turkey, and chicken and all the fixings were put on that table. Victuals were placed on the plates in the kitchen and fetched to the table. Five servants were kept busy refreshing the wedding diners.

Missus Joanna and the Yankee man what she married the day before, her sister, the lady what sang, and her mammy and pappy, and the parson sat at the table what they called the bridal table. That table had the most trimmings on it of bows and ribbons and the like of that. I saw Missus Joanna a-sitting there. She wore her wedding dress just 'zactly like she did the day before, but her face was not covered up. The wedding dinner lasted two hours.

After that, the carriage came around and everybody lined up along the front door by the cape jessamines to throw rice and old shoes at the bride when she came outside to get into the carriage. Everybody was mighty spry to be done danced all the night before until the sun had showed red in the East that morning.

After she was done off, I just couldn't figure out how Marse had gotten so much together for that wedding, because it hadn't been no time since the Yankee soldiers had carried off everything and left him poor. When I turned back to go into the big house, I saw the peafowls a-sneaking off in shame to the river, because they never had a sign of a tail. All their tail feathers were plucked to make the wedding fans and to go in Missus's and Missus Joanna's hats. That sure was the biggest drove of peafowls that ever was, and the folks didn't give them no mind because they didn't have any feathers.

ESAU PERRY
CHAPIN, S. C.

We Did Not Regard Freedom
As An Unmixed Blessing

When I was just a little shaver I was told I belonged to the family of the late Colonel Edward Bookter of upper Fairfield County. I was born in 1849. The Bookter plantation was a big one, with pastures for cattle, hogs, and sheep; big field of cotton, corn, and wheat; and about a dozen African families living on it, mostly out of sight from the Bookter's big house. Two women and three chillun worked in the big house, preparing the food and caring for everything. I was one of the chillun. Marse Colonel Bookter's household had three boys; one bigger than me and two not quite as big as me. We played together, drove up the cows together, and carried on in friendly fashion all the time. The African chillun ate with the servant women in a place fixed for them off from the dining room. We generally had the same food and drink that Marse's family had.

When I was about eleven years old Marse took me to Columbia one Saturday afternoon, and while Marse Colonel Bookter was around at a livery stable on Assembly Street, he gave me some money and told me I could stroll around for a while. I did, and soon found myself with about a dozen of Marse Hampton's boys. As we walked along Gervais Street, we met a big fine looking man with a fishing tackle, going towards the river, and several other folks was with him. As we turned the corner, the big man kind of grinned and said, "Whose boys are you?" The bigger boy with us said, "We all belongs to Marse Hampton." The man reached in his pocket and gave each one of us some money. "Blest if I know my own people anymore," he said.

During the war, and it seemed to me it would never end, we heard much about President Lincoln. I was thirteen years old when President Lincoln set us all free in 1863. The war was still going on and I'm telling you right now that my folks and friends around me did not regard freedom as an unmixed blessing. We didn't know where to go or what to do, and so we stayed right where we were, and there wasn't much difference to our living, because we had always had plenty to eat and wear. I remember my mammy telling me that food was getting scarce, and if any African folks tried to scratch for themselves they would suffer. They'd just take their foot in their hand and ramble about the land like a wolf, she warned.

DANIEL WARING
BOOKTER PLANTATION
FAIRFIELD COUNTY, S. C.

The Payment Of A Shinplaster

Mammy plowed in the field same as Pappy, and I ran along behind, taking the dirt off the cotton plants where the twister plow turned the clods on the plants. When that cotton field got white and red with blooms in summer and white again in the fall, I had to shoulder my poke and go to the field and pick that cotton. The first day I always picked a hundred pounds. Marse Adam Walker, of the Walker Plantation in Chester County, pulled out a big flat black pocketbook and gave me a shinplaster, and said, "Jesse, every time your basket hoists the beam of the steelyard to 100, you get a shinplaster."

Marse lived in a two-story, eight-room house. The kitchen was away from the house. After Christmas, Marse made me the houseboy and I drove the buggy for Missus Eliza when her went visiting. I was fed well and spent my money for a knife, candy, and firecrackers. The Yankees didn't come up as far as Chester. They branched off down about Blackstock, took the sunrise side of that place, and marched on across the Catawba River, at Rocky Mount. I stayed on with Marse Adam and Missus Eliza after freedom.

JESSE WILLIAMS
WALKER PLANTATION
CHESTER COUNTY, S. C.

I Was the Yankees' Cattle Driver

Before freedom, I had a good enough time. Just lay around the house and waited on Marse. I remember when the Yankees came. Been a Sunday morning. They rode up to the gate on horses. Marse happened to come out and I happened to be at the gate. The Yankees took his watch out of his pocket, his pistol which he had girded to him, and they took all the whiskey, catch all chickens and guinea hens, and took them all. Then they went to the lot and took two breeding mares and hitched them to wagon loaded full of corn. They took two carriage horses and hitched them to a carriage and went to the smokehouse and filled the carriage full of sides of meat and ham and shoulders. I been watching to see what else they were going to take. A soldier looked at me and said, "Want to go?" And I rode off behind the two brood mares on the corn.

When they rested that night, I rested right there. It was mighty cold. I suffered a heap in the cold. They gave me a horse, saddled and bridled, and a little bayonet gun. They put me on that horse to drive cattle. When night came, I drove the cattle into a field—anybody's field. Sometimes rain sure fell, and I had to tend to that bunch of cattle, rain or no rain.

General Sherman? I saw him! I remember when I saw him the last time. He had two matched horses going down to Petersburg. Six guards riding by the side of his turnout. Oh, what clothes he had on! He was dressed down in finest uniform.

When I left the Yankees they gave me $35.00. I threw it away eating crackers and peanuts and things like that. And I bought some brogan shoes. I remember it was Sunday morning that General Johnson threw up his hand at Raleigh. Done with the war! After that, I went home.

WILLIS WILLIAMS
CAPE FEAR PLANTATION
ROCK CREEK, S. C.

The Horse's Tail Reached The Ground

Marse Lane had a good house to live in on his plantation. I used to work around the house and in the fields. Mammy was a good seamster and helped the Lanes with their sewing. She taught me to sew and help out too. We didn't get any money for our work. Marse Lane was mean to most of us, but he was good to me. He'd just give me about two licks, but he was mean to Mammy.

We didn't learn to read and write, but some of the Lanes taught Mammy, and she taught me a little bit. On Saturday nights the African people had frolics at their houses, and when someone married, they had a good hot supper. We chillun played all the ole glames like play-ball [throwing over the house], marbles, and base. When we got sick with fever, we were cured with peach tree leaves boiled and drunk. Wild cherry bark was good for most anything if taken at night.

When the Yanks came to the plantation, they took two of the best horses we had. One had a tail that reached the ground. That was the finest horse in the country, and I sure hated to see him go. Marse pulled me up on that horse one time, and it was an honor just to sit on his back.

EMOLINE WILSON
LANE PLANTATION
DUTCH FORK, S. C.

Taking Cotton From Chester To Columbia

About the first thing that stuck in my mind was seeing Marse Charner Scaife a-lying on his bed of death. I felt sorry for everybody then. Missus Mary Rice was mean. She died a year after, and I never felt sad or no ways out of the regular way.

When I was a shaver, I carried water to the rooms and polished shoes for all the folks who lived in the big house. I set the freshly polished shoes at the door of the bedroom. Got a nickel for that and danced for joy over it. Two servant girls cleaned the rooms, and I helped carry out things and take up ashes and fetch wood and build fires early every day.

Marse's house had five bedrooms and a sitting room. The kitchen and dining room were in the back yard. A covered passage kept them from getting wet when they went to the dining room. Marse said he had rather get cold going to eat than to have the food get cold while it was being fetched to him.

I sometimes helped split rails for fences. I didn't have to work on Christmas, and Mammy cooked coffee and biscuit for breakfast.

It took a week to take the cotton boat from Chester to Columbia. Six boat hands—the boatman, two oarsmen, two steermen and an extra man—handled the flatboat. The steermen steered with long poles on the way up the river and paddled down the river. The oarsmen were behind them. They used to pole, too, going up, and they paddled going down.

Seventy-five or eighty bales of cotton were carried at a time. The bales weighed around three hundred pounds apiece.

In Columbia, the wharfs were on the Congaree River banks. The boat was loaded with all kind of things going home—sugar and coffee.

On the Broad River, we passed by Woods Ferry, Fish Dam Ferry, Hendersons Ferry, and Hendersons Island. We unloaded at our own ferry, called Scaife Ferry.

ALEXANDER SCAIFE

The Secret Of The Turkeys

My name is Nina Scott. I worked for Marse Dr. Shipp at Wofford College. Marse Dr. Shipp lived in a big house on the Wofford College campus. He had turkeys, chickens, and pigs. Mammy was the cook, and she made the bestest turkey and dressing you ever tasted. Marse Dr. Shipp just loved Mammy's turkey and dressing. He said she browned down the turkey just right. Sometimes she had to make extra dressing for him, when the dressing ran out before the turkey was gone.

When we heard the Yankees were a-coming, Mammy caught all the turkeys and hid them. At first she didn't want to tell me where they were. I told her I wouldn't tell the Yankees. Finally, she broke down and told me where the big ole gobblers were.

One day Marse Dr. Shipp sent someone to tell me to come to his office. "Nina," he said, "Have you heard that the Yankees are coming?" "Yas, sir," I answered. "They'll take everything they can carry away," Marse said, and I don't want them to take the turkeys. I can be deprived of many things, but I don't want to be deprived of your mother's good turkey and dressing." "Yas, sir," I answered. "Nina, do you know where your mother has taken the turkeys for safekeeping?" he asked. "Yas, sir." "Where are the turkeys, Nina?" "The turkeys are in the woods, near the creek," I said. "Mammy's been feeding them corn, and they have been roosting there."

Marse Dr. Shipp looked at me with fire in his eyes. "Nina, go quickly and tell your mother to hide the turkeys in another place, and tell her not to tell you where they are. *I* don't want to know where the turkeys are being held, and I don't want *you* to know. If we don't know, and your mother doesn't tell, then the Yankees cannot find them and take them away." "Yas, sir. Ill tell Mammy to hide them at another place and not tell me where she hid them."

NINA SCOTT
WOFFORD COLLEGE CAMPUS
SPARTANBURG, S. C.

Going To War With General Hampton

I was born on Marse Hampton's big plantation over in the Mississippi Delta. I never knew what hunger was, and my friends and bosses had me reading, writing, and cyphering right well before I was ten years old.

General Hampton visited his plantation twice a year, in the spring and in the fall. I sure did get to looking forward to his coming. The last time Marse Hampton came was in 1860, and he brought me to Columbia with him. He sure was some busy after we got here, and in a year or two old Marse called me and said, "Ranson, we've got a big war on hand, and I want you to go with me to the front, where we're going to whup the North. I sure was pleased and told him I shoot until I die for him. "No," he said, "Ranson, you ain't going to fight. You are going along to look after me, in case I get hungry or hurt or anything. I need a young boy to take care of me."

Marse Hampton had a million men fighting with him. He was hardly out of one fight 'til he was in another battle. We were always at it, around Richmond. Sometimes in a field and sometimes in the woods, sometimes in the daytime and sometimes after dark. It was like an age of Sundays that Marse General Hampton came to the tent and smiled as he told me, "Well, Ranson, I got as many of them Yankees as they got of me."

One time the Hampton army was fighting at Brandy Station, Virginia, and I saw Marse General Hampton coming on his horse, sitting up straight. He dismounted at the tent and came in. Some of his officers were already there. They saluted and he saluted, and I saw trouble in his face. Then they all shook his hand, and Marse General Hampton said, "It's the price of war. None of us go in knowing whether we ride back ourselves or be hauled back dead." Then they brought the dead body of Colonel Frank Hampton, the General's son.

He had died on the battlefield, falling in action, just like the fine brave boy he was, as he stood six feet two inches, and loved everybody worth loving. That was June 9, 1863, a sad time. It was not long after that 'til Marse General Hampton sent me back to Columbia.

RANSOM SIMMONS
GEN. WADE HAMPTON'S BODY SERVANT
COLUMBIA, S.C.

One Old Woman Was a Witch

I belonged to Marse John Hiller in Lexington County. Old Marse was strict on his African people.

The African people never learned to read and write. If any of them were caught trying to learn to read or write, they were whipped bad. I caught on to what the white chillun said, and learned by myself to say the alphabet.

Before freedom came, the patrollers were strong and whipped anyone they caught without a pass. Wouldn't let you go to church without a pass.

Lots of hunting rabbits, squirrels, foxes and 'possums. And we fished. In the garden we raised potatoes, turnips, collards and peas.

One old woman was a witch, and she rode me one night. I couldn't get up that night, had a catching of my breath and couldn't raise up. She held me down. There were lots of fevers in them days, and they were cured with root herbs and barks.

When the Yankees came through, burning, killing, and stealing the stock, I was in Marse's yard. They grabbed Marse and hit him. Then they burned his house, stole the stock, and one Yankee stuck his sword to my breast and said for me to come with him or he would kill me. Of course I went along. They took me as far as the Broad River, on the other side of Chapin. They turned me loose and told me to run fast and not to go back to that old Marse. I found my way back home by watching the sun.

SAM RAWLS
JOHN HILLER PLANTATION
LEXINGTON COUNTY, S. C.

A Horse Named Beauty

I was a little boy to be driving such big cows. Missus Cum and Missus Lizzie Rice were Marse Alex's sisters. Marse Alex done died, and they were my Missuses. When the overseer, Jim Blalock, try to act rough, out of Missuses' sight, they found out and set him down a peg.

My shirts were made on the looms. I wore long shirts and went outside in my shirttail. I kept clean, too, cause Missus never liked no dirt around her.

Three hundred hogs had to be attended to, two hundred yearlings and heifers, and Lordy knows how many sheep and goats. We kept them fat. When butchering time came, we stewed out the mostest lard and we had enough side meat to supply the plantation the year around.

Our wheat land was fertilized with load after load of cotton seed. The wheat we raised was the talk of the countryside. Besides that, there was rye, oats, and barley, and I ain't said nothing about the bottom corn that lay in the cribs from year to year.

The fattest of all the horses was Missus's black saddle horse called Beauty. My missus wore the longest sidesaddle dress that hung way down below her feets. Somebody always had to help her on and off Beauty, but not one of her brothers could outride Missus.

PHILLIP RICE
RICE PLANTATION
UNION, S. C.

The Pot Of Gold

Mammy was African. Pappy was a Native American Indian. Pappy sometimes made a little money showing people how to make Indian medicine that was good for their complaints and how to kill their hogs according to the moon. He told us many times about the great Catawba Indians who made all their own medicines and killed bears and dressed in bear skins after feasting on their flesh. Pappy was a good talker. One day he left home, and he never came back.

Mammy kept busy cooking, nursing, and washing, and we chillun helped. Two brothers were older than me and a little baby brother was about a year old. Mammy was home one day when my brothers and me was chopping cotton in the field. We chopped 'til about eleven o'clock that morning. One of my brothers said, "When we get to the big oak tree, we'll sit down and rest." We chillun liked each other and we joked and worked fast until we came to the end of the rows and the shade of the big oak.

My oldest brother and me sat down, and my other brother was a little behind us in his chopping. As he neared the finish, his hoe hit something hard and it rang. He raked the dirt away and kept digging. "What you doing, brother?" I asked. He said, "Trying to find out what this is. It seems to be a pot lid." Then we jumped up and went to him and all of us pulled dirt away and sure enough it was a pot lid and it was on a pot. We dug it out, thinking it would be a good thing to take home. It was so heavy it took all three of us to dig it out.

No sooner was the pot out of the ground than we took off the lid and we were sure surprised at what we saw. Big silver coins lay all over the top. We took two of them and dropped them together and they rang. Then we grabbled in the pot for more. The silver went down about two fingers deep. Gold pieces ran down about four fingers or so.

We walked to the house feeling pretty big and my oldest brother was singing, "Hawk and buzzard went to the law; the hawk came back with a broken jaw." Mammy looked at us and said: "What you all coming to dinner so soon for?" Then she looked up and saw the pot and said, "Land sakes, what you all got?" We put the big pot down in the middle of the floor and took off the lid, and Mammy said, "Oh! Let's see what we has." She began to empty the pot and to count the coins. She told us to watch the door and see that nobody got in, 'cause she was not at home! She made us swear we not say nothing about finding the pot of gold. She would see what she could find out about it.

Some weeks after that, she told us she heard about someone who had buried some money and went to the war without telling anybody where the money was. Maybe he was killed and that was all we would ever know about him. Mammy kept it and we all worked on just the same and she kept the money for a long time.

After we moved to Columbia, Mammy said the pot of gold was worth $5,700. She bought two lots on Senate Street, built a two-story house, and had rent money coming in.

MARTHA RICHARDSON
COLUMBIA, S. C.

Singing The Old Song

I was born fourteen miles north of Chester, on the plantation of Missus Rebecca Nance. Pappy was Baker. Mammy was Mary. Pappy was bought out of a drove of African people from Virginia. Mammy was born on the Youngblood Plantation. Youngblood was the name of Missus' people who lived in York County.

Pappy lived three miles from the plantation where Mammy lived. He could only visit her on a written pass. As he was religiously inclined, dutiful and faithful as a worker, Mammy encouraged the relation that included a marriage between Pappy and Mammy.

Mammy had a log house for us. Beds were made by the plantation carpenter. I plowed from sun to sun, with an hour for dinner and feeding the horses.

Marse and Missus gave us three-cent pieces, and once or twice, dimes. I used them to buy firecrackers and candy. When we were sick Missus visited us and summoned a doctor the first thing. The remedies were castor oil, quinine, turpentine, mustard plaster and bleeding.

We began to hear whispers that freedom might come. The women who worked in the big house picked up everything they heard and passed it on to us in the quarters. I went around singing Mammy's song: "'Possum up the 'simmon tree; sparrow on the ground. 'Possum throw the 'simmons down; sparrow shake them 'round."

I have never been so frightened as I was when I heard that Marse was going off to the war. The evening before he went, a whippoorwill lighted on a windowsill at the big house and uttered the sound, "Whip-poor-will." All the Africans on the place heard about it and were frightened and awed and predicted bad luck to Marse Will. It seemed to be an omen. Marse Will left for the war.

Toward the end of the struggle, we heard that he had taken sick.

Someone said he had wasted away. He was brought home in rags and died. Missus gave us Africans a big dinner on New Year's Day and talked to us out of the catechism. She impressed on us that we were free. Most were silent and glad.

BENJAMIN RUSSELL
REBECCA NANCE PLANTATION
CHESTER, S. C.

The Castor Oil Bottle

I belonged to Marse Tom Rabb. Marse Tom's hair was jet black and even when he shaved, whisker roots were so black his face appeared black. I come to birth on his place two or three miles from Monticello in the country. They say President Buchanan was president, though I don't know about that.

Pappy was Henry. Mammy was Ella. She was the cook at the big house. I was too little to work and I just hung around the kitchen, toting water and picking up chips. Since Mammy was the cook, I was right there at her apron strings all the time and I ate what the Marse and Missus ate. I did!

Those that had not been good or done something bad were kept at home on Sunday and the people who had been good went to church.

When I got sick, they fanned me and kept off the flies. They were particular about sickness. They had a time with some chillun and the castor oil bottle, I tell you. You had to take medicine according to the doctor's orders, and that meant castor oil.

ELLA KELLY
RABB PLANTATION
MONTICELLO, S. C.

Children Ate From A Trough

Marse fed us African chillun in a trough in the yard. He had his own smokehouse where he cured his meat. His flour was ground in the neighborhood. Sometimes he allowed a family in the quarters of have a patch to plant watermelons in. In our garden, we planted by the signs. Potatoes, turnips, and sweet potatoes were planted in the dark of the moon, while beans were planted in the sign of the crawfish. But we ate in a trough, just like hogs.

I was a girl but I had to split rails and dig ditches just like boy chillun and men. After that, I worked in the cotton fields. I went home at night and went to bed to rest. I worked all day on Saturday, but never worked on Sunday. I had Christmas day off.

Pappy was Richard and Mammy was Martha. We wore heavy brogan shoes with brass toes. Mammy worked at the big house, carding, spinning, and weaving the cloth. She made dye from mud, and if she wanted gray she used tree bark. For brown dye she used walnut tree bark.

MARY JANE KELLY
BROAD RIVER SECTION, S. C.

The Yankees Came Two-By-Two

I was a boy and I know how them rice fields come about. It was like this: All them rice fields been nothing but swamps. African people cut kennel and cut down woods and dig ditch through raw woods. All been cleared up for to plant rice.

I remember the Yankee boats coming up the Waccamaw River to Mont Arena Plantation on Sandy Island. Gunboats, about ten o'clock in the morning. Soldiers all mustered out and scattered all over the island, came two by two, guns on their shoulders, glistening against the sun. Blue coats, blue pants, hats all blue. They broke in the barn, stole rations from us African people, took hogs, geese, ducks.

My grandpappy, Nelson Lance, was the driver for Marse Francis Withers Heriot on Sandy Island. Marse went to swamp. Hid in the woods. Grandpappy took old Missus Sally Heriot on his back and hid her in the woods. She couldn't walk because of the rheumatism.

The Yankees stayed but the one day. Ravaged all over the island. All goats, hogs, chickens, ducks, geese—all the animals but one cow—been taken on the Yankee gunboats. Yankees broke into Marse's big rice barn and shared all that out to the African folks in the quarters.

Some of the people in the quarters ran away from Sandy Island. Went to the seashore and took rowboat and gone out and joined with the Yankees. That crowd never came back.

Anybody who ran away or didn't do task was put in barn, and they gave them twenty-five to fifty lashes. Gave them less rations to boot. Cut them down to one quart of molasses, one pound of meat, and one peck of corn for a week.

GABE LANCE
MONT ARENA PLANTATION
SANDY ISLAND, S. C.

Golliwhopshus Names

I was born in the southeast corner of Winnsboro on the Clifton Plantation. The day I was born the plantation belonged to Marse David Gaillard and Missus Louisa. One day Missus Louisa said, "Ned, don't you ever call my husband 'Old Marse,' and don't you ever think of me as 'Old Missus.'" I promised her I would always keep that in mind, and I ain't gonna change although she went to heaven and is in the choir singing them chants that she could pipe so pretty at St. Johns in Winnsboro.

They were Episcopalians. There was no hard shell Baptist and no soft shell Methodist in their makeup. It was all glory, big glory, glory in the highest rung on Jacob's ladder.

Now Marse David and Missus Louisa had a plantation down on the Santee, in the Low Country, but I didn't go down there. The quarters on our plantation was a little town laid out with streets wide enough for a wagon to pass through. Houses were on each side of the street. A well and church was in the center of the town. There was a gin, barns, stables, cowpen and a big bell on top of a high pole at the barn gate. A big trough was at the well, and it was kept full of water, day and night, in case of fire.

Marse didn't 'low chillun to be worked. We had pumpkin pie on Sunday. No butter, no sweet milk, but we got clabber and buttermilk.

When 'mancipation came, the plantation belonged to Marse Henry, a grandson of Marse David, and Marse Henry ladled out some golliwhopshus names that day, such as, Caesar Harrison, Edward Cades, and Louis Brevard. He said, "Louis, I give you the name of a judge. Dan, I give you a Roman name, Pompey. He gave Uncle Sam the name of Shadrack. When he reached Uncle Aleck, he 'lowed as how he would add two fine names to Aleck: names of a preacher and a scholar, Porter Ramsey.

NED WALKER
CLIFTON PLANTATION
WINNSBORO, S. C.

The Ghost

Marse was John and Missus was Betsy. Missus was mighty particular about our religion. I absorbed all I have in me from Missus, I really believe. She was kind and gentle, and she moved among us like a living benediction. Many were the blessings that fell from her hands for the sick and afflicted. She got tired, but I never saw her too weary to go to a crying child or a moaning grown person. We were obliged to love her, because she knew us more better than we knew ourselves. More than that, she had her sons' wives teach us how to read, write, and figure enough to help us.

One day I went down the road whistling with nothing on my mind. I saw a woman with a basket on her arm coming toward me. I raised my hand to speak but I ain't seen that woman no more. I stopped and looked everywhere and there was nobody in that road except me. A peculiar feeling crept over my body. I had been looking for hants and spirits that the older folks talked about and I ain't never seen one before this one.

I tore off down the road faster than a wild horse. I cut across the field towards a narrow strip of woods close to home. When my foots hit the rough grass and corn stalks of the field they took hold and worked like a wheel. I glanced back to see what it was and before I could turn around again I smacked my head into a pine tree. My running ceased right there. A breeze fanned my face, and then everything got still.

Next morning when my mind came back to me, the sun was shining straight in my face. I lay there on the ground blinking my eyes, wondering if I was still living. I tried to move and sure enough I was there all right.

Marse and Missus died soon after the war and my family went to live with young Marse and Missus on a plantation on the other side of the Saluda River.

WALTER LONG
LONG PLANTATION
LEXINGTON S. C.

The Little Runt Was Called Tom Shanty

I belonged to Marse Robin Brice. Missus's name was Missus Jennie. Marse and Missus's chillun were Marse John, Marse Chris, and Marse Tom. Marse Tom been a little runt, and they called him Tom Shanty.

Mammy worked with the cows, and she churned the milk and made butter. I helped her with the cows, calves, and churning. We had all that milk 'round all the time. I ran my fingers around the jar where the cream was clinging, and sucked it off my fingers. That was the best thing. Marse and Missus lived in a big two-story house. We lived in a little log house, with log chimneys.

I wore an asafetida bag around my neck to keep off croup, measles, diphtheria, and whooping cough. Marse sent for Dr. Walter Brice when I got very ill.

Pappy belonged to Marse John Partook Brice, and Mammy belonged to Marse Robin. Pappy had to have a pass to come to see us.

BEN LEITNE
BRICE PLANTATION
WINNSBORO, S. C.

I Was One of the Fire Boys

I, Mike Lawrence, belonged to what was called "the Murray state." I was one of Major William Meggett Murray's "fire boys," who was charged with the specific duty of bringing live coals to Marse Murray whenever he wanted to light his pipe.

I remember this that happened on Fenwick Island: When Old John ain't showed up on Saturday morning, his Marse asked everybody where he been and the people all banded together and told Marse that they saw him leave in a boat to go fishing and he ain't been seen since. Marse been worry sure 'nough then, 'cause he thought John might have drowned.

Marse engaged four men to shoot gun all over the creek to make John's body rise. The body didn't rise. After that, they dragged all about in the gutters. Marse went to bed with a heavy heart 'cause he been very fond of Old John.

John came back to Fenwick Island early on Monday morning and 'fore dayclean he cut the fence rails. Now, one hundred rails been called a good day's work, but Old John decided he was going to do better than that. He found five trees growing close together, and he cut a piece out of every one. Then he chopped at the biggest tree until it fell, and that tree knocked all the rest over.

When all the trees fell together, it made such a noise, that Marse heard it when he was still in his bed, and he hastened to dress so he could see what was going on in the woods. He saddled the horse and rode until he got to the center of the noise and there he saw John cutting away like he was crazy.

Marse been mad sure enough, but then he was glad to see that John ain't been drowned. He started to say something, but John interrupted and sang out, "Go away Marse, I ain't got time to talk with you now."

John then gathered up five axes and went to the five trees laying down on the ground. He drove the axe in every tree and then grabbed a heavy maul. While Marse was looking on, he took the maul and ran from one tree to another and as quick as he swung the axe, the tree split wide open. Marse started to say something, but again John ain't let him talk. He said, "Go on home, Marse."

Marse went on home without a word. When he went back in the woods that evening, he checked up and found that Old John had done cut five hundred rails. Old John was a man, I tell you.

EPHRIAM (MIKE) LAWRENCE
MURRAY PLANTATION
EDISTO ISLAND, S. C.

The Man Who Ran Away

I was about seven years old. Most of the African people went right along doing their chores, as expected of them, but a few were restless, and they broke the rules by running about without asking. And always there were some who tried to escape by going far away to the North.

One big African man stole away one night from Marse's plantation and got to Charleston. He got on a boat and was going to run away, but the overseer caught up with him. The runaway said to the overseer, "I tried to get away from the plantation. I was going to Massachusetts and hire out until I got enough to carry me back to my home in Africa."

When someone tried to run away like that, it was the custom to have a trial, and Marse and Missus went to the trial to listen and to ask the person being tried some questions. Missus attended this trial, and she said to all the others there, "Put yourself in this man's shoes, and what would you do? The best way to treat such a man is to be kind and patient with him and he will forget his old home." The man was led away and I never did hear if he was whipped.

Pappy went away to the war and Mammy and me stayed in our cabin alone. She cried and wondered where he was, if he was well, or if he had been killed. One day we heard that he was dead. Mammy, too, passed in a short time.

When Sherman's army came through Fairfield County, I saw them riding by for hours. Some of them carried balls in their hands, which they threw against houses to make them explode and burn. I have always suspected that is just the way they set the houses afire when Columbia was burned in a single night. Some of the houses in Fairfield County were burned, some in Winnsboro, and others in the country, but Columbia was the only place that was wiped out.

As the army passed, all us Africans stood by the side of the road and cried and asked them not to burn our Marse and Missus's house, and they didn't. The man who had tried to run away to Africa was the first one to pick up his hat and laugh out loud when President Lincoln set all the Africans free in January, 1863. The man who had been tried for trying to run away said, "Now I go, thank the Lord." And he struck right out, but he did not get much beyond the barn, when he turned and came back.

He walked in the yard to the big house and he saw Missus looking at him. He took off his hat and bowed low and said, "Missus, I'm so happy to be free that I forgot myself, but I will not leave until you say so. I will not leave you when you need a hand." Missus looked down and she saw the man, so big and strong, with tears flowing down his cheeks. She said, "You are a good worker and you have suffered much. Make yourself at home just as you have been doing, and when you want to go far away, come to me, and I'll see that you get enough money to pay your way to Boston and maybe to Africa." And that is what happened two years later.

AMIE LUMPKIN
MOBLEY PLANTATION
FAIRFIELD COUNTY, S. C.

I Thought Judgment Day Had Come

I was little but I soon learned to make lye soap. We put up the hopper. That meant hanging up strong ash wood and hickory ashes in a bag that was wet, so the lye would drip down into a box where soap was made. When a hopper was made, it was in a V shape, with a trough underneath for the drippings. To make soap you had to have pork grease.

When the moon got right, the grease was boiled off the bones and put in the lye that had dripped from the wood ashes. Then it was cooked up into soap. Soap was made on the increase of the moon, and only a sassafras stick was used for stirring. The soap maker stirred all the time.

If the soap was too strong when you took a bath, your skin would come off. Hard soap was used for washing, and soft soap for clothes.

Another thing we did with lye was to shell corn and put the grains in lye and clean it. When it came white, we called it "hominy."

We had so many ups and downs, and the overseer was hard on us, too. I was old enough to sleep by myself, and tried to stand well with all the peoples and God.

I was still little when the war came, but I can remember when the horn blew, telling us that the war was done over and we were free. I thought Judgment Day had come!

EISON LYLES
LYLES PLANTATION
NEWBERRY, S. C.

Mother And Son Reunited

I was born in Limestone, Virginia. I was sold when I was ten years old. The paper on me was a kind of mortgage. That is when I came to South Carolina. Mammy was Jane, and she came to South Carolina too. We got back together again at Orangeburg, at Marse Captain Cherry's plantation near Charleston.

Pappy was Tony, a carriage driver. He wore his tall hat and fine livery clothes and he was a musicianer, playing violin at the Academy on the old Ninety-Six Road. All the Marses and Missuses educated their chillun there, and they attended parties there. Oh, the beautifulest ladies—they wore long dresses and had long hair. Pappy always played violin at the parties.

My great-grandpappy was an Indian chief, Cherokee, Kickapoo, I don't remember. I had a task, and I did my task and I helped others with their task so they wouldn't get whipped. My task was to roll the carpet for Missus to get in the carriage. A two-foot carpet was rolled from the house to the stoop for the carriage. Mammy's task was to fix the flowers. She would take this little flower and that little flower, and put them together and make up a beautiful bouquet. Pappy knew all about planting. The people would come to ask him how to plant this and when to plant that.

RICHARD MACK
CHERRY PLANTATION
ORANGEBURG, S. C.

Caught With Sugar Cane

I was born on the Lord's Day. Marse was Wateree Jim McCrorey. Missus was Sara. Pappy was named Washington, after General George Washington, though he got nothing but "Wash" in the handling of his name. Mammy was Dolly, after the President's wife, Dolly. Marse and Missus told Mammy that she was named for a very great lady. I liked best to eat 'lasses and pone bread for breakfast; roastin' ears, string beans, hog jowls, and bread and buttermilk for dinner; and clabber and blackberry cobbler for supper. That's good eatin's I tell you.

I was too young to work much, but I tended to the cows, carried water to the fields, picked up chips, and found the turkey and guinea nests. I remembers once on a moonlight night about midnight. I got up off my pallet on the floor and went out in the sugar cane patch and got a big stalk of the cane.

When I got back to our house, young Marse, son of Marse Wateree Jim McCrorey, ketch me and say, "That you?" I'd like to deny it was me, but there I was, ketched with the cane on me. What could I say? I just say please, Marse Jim, don't tell old Marse. He made his face grim and he said, "Ten lashes and privilege of eating the cane, or five lashes and the cane be given to the pigs in the pen, the lashes to be applied on the bare back and rump."

That last word seemed to tickle him and he laughed. "Which are you going to take?" I said I wanted to eat the sugar cane, but please, young Marse, make the lashes soft as you can. Then he got stern again, took me by the hand, led me to the harness house, and said, "Now, don't you bellow. You might wake Mother." Then he gave me the ten lashes and they weren't soft a-tall. I didn't cry out on the night wind though.

ED MCCROREY
WATEREE PLANTATION, S. C.

A Woman Was Hanged

The overseer blew his horn for us to go to work at sunrise. He gave us a task to do and if you didn't do it, he put a little thing to you. That was a leather lash or some kind of a whip. They didn't have no jails, but an old woman named Peggy was hanged on the galleries [gallows]. They hanged her up by the neck, and the harness broke her neck for wrongdoing, like killing somebody or trying to kill them. She worked for the Scotts, and she tried to poison the Scotts. They were mean to her, she said, and she put poison in their coffee.

Mammy walked about ten miles to see that hanging 'cause they turned all the Africans loose to go to a hanging. Mammy said Peggy was sitting on her coffin. After the hanging, she was placed in the coffin.

I ran away one time and somehow or other the overseer knew where I was. He brought me back, and Missus tied me to the tester bedstead and whipped me 'til the whip broke. Another time, Marse had an apple tree that had only one apple on it and he wanted to save that apple until it got ripe enough for the seed. I couldn't stand it. I ate that apple. I couldn't get out of it. I tell you it was a hard time to be up against.

Then the Yankees gave us to understand that we were free.

JAKE McLEOD
McLEOD PLANTATION
MARION, S. C.

No Interest In Worryment

You see, I was just a little gal. I can't lie and say I remember. I been just 'bout so high. I ain't had no reason to study 'bout it and press it on my mind. Mammy died when I was a baby. She was the seamster for our people. Missus promise Mammy to take care of me. The first crack out of me that passed through that window sash Missus came to find out what ailed me.

I hardly missed Mammy. No mammy couldn't treat me better that I was treated. I belonged to Missus Reese Ford who lived at Waterford Plantation on the Black River in Georgetown County.

I don't know nothing 'bout the war. I was protected and taken to the city. I had nothing to bother my mind and make me remember those days. I was spoiled and didn't have no interest in worryment. I don't know nothing 'bout the street on the plantation, and what they did there, 'cause I ain't had no occasion for to go there. I didn't wear the kind of clothes the other chillun wore, and I got my dinner from the kitchen. I don't know nothing 'bout crops 'cause we summered at Plantersville [a resort frequented by the planters of the day]. I just stayed in the yard, and sometimes I took notes around.

I ain't had no kinnery to help me, and I tell you I was spoiled.

ABBEY MISHOW
WATERFORD PLANTATION
BLACK RIVER, S. C.

Married At Fifteen

I was born on the Gladney Plantation. Pappy was George Stitt. Mammy was Phillis Gladney. Pappy worked for the Stitt family and had to get a pass to come to see Mammy. He slipped in and out enough times to have four chillun. Then the Stitts took a notion to sell him to Arkansas.

Mammy weep 'bout that but what could her do? Just nothing. Marse said, "Plenty more good fish in the sea, Phillis. Look 'round, set your cap, and maybe you'll attract one that'll give your heart comfort by and by. Mammy took up with a no-account man name of Bill James and had one child, a boy, named Jim.

How us get fire? Us get two flint rocks, hold lint cotton under them, strike a spark, it drop down, set the cotton afire, and then us fan it to a blaze. Us had just enough clothes to hide our secret parts in summer. A shirt for the boys and a slip-over for the gals. They was made out of weaved cloth that us spinned of the cotton that us picked out of the field. Us raised our own chickens and sang while us worked.

Us went to Jackson Creek Church, Lebanon. The gallery was all 'round the upstairs. One Sunday I went to sleep and snored loud I tell you. When I got home, I got a whipping. Marse and Missus were particular about the preacher. Him come 'round and they fill up the back of his buggy with something of everything on the place: ham, chickens, eggs, butter, marmalade, jelly, 'lasses, sugar, vegetables, and fruit. Him put in full time on Sunday though, preached 'bout two hours before he put on the benediction.

When I was fifteen, I married Bill Moore. Stood up with him that day in a blue worsted dress and a red balmoral over a white tucked petticoat, and under that, a soft pique chemise with no sleeves. Had on white stockings and low quarter shoes. I had sweet shrubs all through my hair and it held them all night and the next night, too. Bill made a big laugh 'bout it, while nosing in my hair and smelling them sweet shrubs.

SENA MOORE
GLADNEY PLANTATION
FAIRFIELD COUNTY, S. C.

Freedom Was A Great Gift

Pappy was Moses Mitchell and Mammy was Tyra. We belonged to Marse John Chaplin and lived on Woodlawn Plantation on Lady's Island. Marse had seven plantations. He lived at Brickyard Plantation in winter and in Beaufort in summer. He had many enslaved Africans, but I don't know how many.

As near as I can remember, there were fifteen Africans on Woodlawn Plantation. We lived on the street. Each cabin had two rooms. Marse didn't give you nothing for your house—you had to get that the best way you could. In our house was bed, table, and bench to sit on. Pappy made them. Mammy had fourteen chillun. We slept on the floor. Every Tuesday Marse gave each worker a peck of corn. When potatoes were dug, we got potatoes. Two times in the year we got six yards of cloth, calico in spring and homespun in the winter. Once a year we got shoes.

Pappy had a boat and he went fishing at night and sold fish. Marse let him cut posts and wood at night and sell that, too. Pappy did his work at night 'cause in daytime he had to do his task. He was carpenter, but when there was no carpentry work on the plantation, he plowed. Mammy hoed. Little boys and old men minded the cows; little girls and old women minded babies. Little chillun played in mud pie and made house of sand and such things.

I started to mind the cows when I was nine years old. When I was twelve I started work in the field and cutting marsh grass and splitting rails.

On Woodlawn there was no overseer. Marse didn't allow much whipping, but workers had to do task. If you didn't, then you got a whipping. Driver did the whipping, but if he whipped too severely, Marse would sometimes take a field hand and make him the driver and put the driver in the field.

When we were sick, Marse would come and see what was the matter. Sometimes he would give us jollip to make us vomit, sometimes if we had fever, he would give us hippo. If we were very sick, Marse would take us to Beaufort to the doctor. If a woman got sick, Missus would go and see her.

We had only one holiday in the year, and that was Christmas Day. Marse killed a cow on every plantation on Christmas and gave all the Africans some.

We had to tell Marse when we got ready to court. If Marse said "No, you can't marry that gal, then that settled it." He didn't like for his slaves to marry slaves on another person's plantation, but if you did that then you had to get a pass to visit your wife. A white preacher came to Marse's house to do the marrying.

We had our own church on the plantation with an African preacher, but on Communion Sunday we had to go to the white folks' church in Beaufort and sit upstairs. We could go to Beaufort on Saturday night, but had to be back by 9 o'clock or a patroller would get us.

Abraham Lincoln was the president of the United States. He came to Beaufort and ate dinner at Colonel Paul Hamilton's house at the Oaks. Marse Lincoln left his gold-headed walking cane there and nobody knew the president of the United States had been to Beaufort 'til he wrote back and told them to look behind the door and send him his gold-handled walking cane.

That Wednesday in November when gun first shoot at Bay Point, I thought it was thunder rolling, but there wasn't no cloud. Mammy said, "Son, that ain't no thunder. That's the Yankee come to give you your freedom." I been so glad that I jumped up and down and ran around. Pappy been splitting rails and Marse came from Beaufort in the carriage and tore by him yelling for Pappy. He told Pappy to get Marse's eight-oar boat named *The Terrify* and carry him to Charleston. Pappy ran to the house and told Mammy what Marse said. Mammy said, "You ain't gonna row no boat to Charleston. You go out that back door and keep a-going. Pappy did, and Marse got some other man to row him and his family to Charleston.

After Freedom came the Yankee opened schools for the Africans and the teachers lived in Marse's big house at Brickyard Plantation. Pappy got a job as carpenter with the Yankees and bought ten acres of land on Lady's Island. I think freedom was a great gift. I liked Marse and I guess he was as good to us as he could be, but I would rather be free.

SAM MITCHELL
WOODLAWN PLANTATION
LADY'S ISLAND, S. C.

GLOSSARY

andirons	metal supports for logs in a fireplace
antebellum	before the Civil War
ape	to look at
asafetida	a gum resin from the roots of several plants
ash cake	cake baked in ashes
bale	a large, tightly compressed, bundle of cotton
balmoral	a brimless Scottish cap with a flat top
beaver	a flat, round hat decorated with beaver fur
bee gum	bee hive, artificial shelter for honey bees
big house	plantation manor house
biggity	intolerant
blacksmith	a person who makes horseshoes
bleeding	drawing blood from a person
boneset	a plant believed to have healing properties, of the genus Eupatorium
bound to	worked for
bow and scrape	yield in judgment and opinion
breastworks	a hastily constructed fort, usually breast high
buccaneer	pirate
buckra	white people
Bull Run	place where major Civil War battles were fought in 1861 and 1862
callous	hardened skin
candy 'taters	candied yams
carding	process wherein fibers yield to sliver form

catechism	a summary of principles of a Christian religion
census	registration of citizens
chat	conversation
chemise	a woman's loose-fitting undergarment
chillun	children
crib	a bin for storing grain
cooling board	a piece of timber immediately free of heat on which a corpse is placed before being buried
crackling bread	bread containing crisp, brown skin of a hog
crave	long for, desire eagerly
cup and saddled	a method by which logs are connected: an oval shaped space is chipped out of a log into which another log is fitted
Custom House	a seaport building where goods and merchandise are collected and vessels are cleared
dayclean	daybreak
diphtheria	an infectious disease
driver	overseer
eggnog	a drink made of eggs, milk and cream
epitaph	an inscription on a tombstone
fare	to get along
fatback	fat meat from the upper part of a side of pork
fetch	to go for and bring back
firedogs	supports for logs
flatboat	a flat-bottomed boat
flax	a plant cultivated for its flower and seeds
flyin' 'round	courting

fodder	coarse food for livestock
frock	a dress
furlough	vacation granted to an enlisted man
galleries	gallows
gallery	a balcony
gin house	a building where seeds are removed from cotton fibers
girded	bound
golliswhopshus	fantastic
grabble	feel or search with the hands
grist mill	a place where grain is ground
Hampton, Wade	Confederate general and U.S. senator, 1818-1902
hand	a worker
hant	a ghost
hearsay	unofficial information gained from another person
heifer	a cow under three years of age that has never produced a calf
highfalutin	haughty, pretentious
hippo	a syringe that injected medicine under the skin
hoe cake	cake made with cornmeal, baked on a hoe
hog jowl	hog jaw
hoop skirt	a woman's skirt made to flare out in bell shape by a framework of flexible hoops
houseboy	a boy who did odd jobs in the big house
indigo	a plant grown on the plantations from which blue dye was made

infair	a time of feasting
jiffy	hurry
jollip	something used to induce vomiting
kennel	a canal
kinnery	relatives
lard	the rendered fat of hogs
'lasses	molasses, a thick, dark-colored syrup
lick	whip
liniment	liquid preparation rubbed on skin, for bruises
locust beer	a beverage made from leaves of a locust tree
loom	a hand-operated apparatus for weaving fabric
mammy	mother
mancipation	emancipation
marse	the master of the plantation
maul	a heavy hammer
'membrance	remembrance
miasma	poisonous germs infecting the atmosphere
milliner	a person who designs and makes hats for women
mint julep	a frosted drink garnished with sprigs of mint
missus	the master's wife
mortgage	a conveyance of property to a creditor as security
mull	soft, thin muslin
mussel	an edible freshwater clam
numerator	someone who counted the Africans
omen	an event believed to forewarn of evil
overseer	a man in charge of the Africans

pappy	father
pass	a paper giving permission to cross a property line
passel	a group
patchety	patched, held together or repaired with patches
patrollers	men who patrolled the plantation to maintain security
peafowl	peacock
petticoat	an underskirt
piddle	to waste time
pique	a cotton fabric
pitch	a crude turpentine that exudes from the bark of pines
plaited	braided
plank floors	floors made of wood planks or boards
poke	a bag
pone bread	baked bread made of cornmeal
pot liquor	the liquid left in the pot after the food has been boiled
providence	a divine being, God
quarters	the street of houses in which the Africans lived
ransack	search
rations	rice, flour, salt, and other food
refuged	having taken refuge at a safe place
right smart	plenty
saddle bags	bags of medical supplies
salve	a medical ointment for healing

scythe	an implement consisting of a curving blade
seamster	a seamstress
shaver	a child
shinplaster	paper money of a denomination lower than one dollar
shirttail	wearing only a skirt
shuttle	a device for passing cloth from one side of a machine to another
side meat	salt pork and bacon taken from sides of a hog
signs	occurrences or objects that give evidence of an event
'simmon beer	a beverage made from persimmons
sitting room	a small living room
skedaddle	run away hurriedly
somersault	an acrobatic movement, the body turning end over end
'spect	expect
'spicious	suspicious
spinning	process of converting fibrous material into thread
spirit	God
stamping ground	homeplace
steelyard	a portable weighing device
stubble	stalks left in the ground
swelled	rose over the bank (a creek or river)
syllabub	a drink made of milk and cider
tan	convert animal hide into leather
tannery	a place where hide is converted to leather

task	a specific piece of work assigned to a person
teas	hot tea made from herbs, roots, leaves, etc.
teeny	small
tester	a canopy over a bed
ticking	a strong cotton fabric
'ticular	particular
toted	carried
trough	boxlike receptacle to hold water or food for animals
turnout	an outfit of clothing
underground railroad	a system of cooperation between persons opposed to slavery who secretly helped fugitive slaves escape to Canada or other places of safety
victuals	food
Waterloo	Belgium city where Napoleon was defeated in 1815
weave	make fabric, cloth
Wheeler, Joseph	Civil War cavalry general
whup	to whip
worryment	worry, concern
worsted	wool cloth woven with a hard smooth surface
yarn	thread made for weaving
yearling	a one-year-old horse

Bibliography

Slave Narratives: A Folk History of Slavery in the United States from Interviews with Former Slaves. Typewritten records prepared by the Federal Writers' Project, 1936–1938. On file at the South Caroliniana Library, University of South Carolina, Columbia, South Carolina, and the Library of Congress, Washington, D.C.

Childs, Arney R., ed. *Rice Planter and Sportsman: The Recollections of J. Motte Alston, 1821–1909.* Columbia: University of South Carolina Press, 1953.

Joyner, Charles. *Remember Me: Slave Life in Coastal Georgia.* Atlanta: Georgia Humanities Council, Georgia History and Culture Series, 1989.

Joyner, Charles. *Down by the Riverside: A South Carolina Slave Community.* Urbana and Chicago: University of Illinois Press, 1984.

Pringle, Elizabeth W. Allston. *Chronicles of "Chicora Wood."* New York: Scribners, 1922.

Rhyne, Nancy. *John Henry Rutledge: The Ghost of Hampton Plantation.* Orangeburg, South Carolina: Sandlapper Publishing Co., Inc., 1997.

A wealth of information on Carolina enslaved African children can be obtained at the Penn Center, on St. Helena Island, and the Avery Research Center, a division of the College of Charleston.

About the Author

Native North Carolinian **Nancy Rhyne** has called coastal South Carolina home for many years. Today, she resides in Myrtle Beach with her husband, Sid.

A popular storyteller and author, Nancy is a much-sought-after speaker. She divides her time between writing, research, and personal appearance. Her great interest in Low Country oral history has kept her on the road for weeks at a time. Through Nancy's writing, the reader is introduced to the beliefs, traditions, and history of the people of this unique area of the southern United States.

Other Books by Nancy Rhyne
Alice Flagg: The Ghost of the Hermitage
Carolina Seashells
Chronicles of the South Carolina Sea Islands
Coastal Ghosts
The Jack-O'-Lantern Ghost
John Henry Rutledge: The Ghost of Hampton Plantation
More Tales of the South Carolina Low Country
Murder in the Carolinas
Once Upon a Time on a Plantation
The South Carolina Lizard Man
Southern Recipes and Legends
Tales of the South Carolina Low Country
Touring Coastal Georgia Backroads
Touring Coastal South Carolina Backroads